Visions of the Prophet

By the same author

THE EYE OF THE PROPHET
(Translated by Margaret Crosland)

Visions of the Prophet

KAHLIL GIBRAN

Translated from the French by
Margaret Crosland

SOUVENIR PRESS

To Él . . . ise
who will emerge
from among our readers
to prolong our desire

This book is a translated selection of writings from
Visions du Prophète by Kahlil Gibran, published in
France by Éditions du Rocher.
Adaptation française réalisée par M. Dahdah,
Copyright © Éditions du Rocher 1995

English translation Copyright © 1996
by Souvenir Press and Margaret Crosland

First English edition published 1996 by
Souvenir Press Ltd, 43 Great Russell Street,
London WC1B 3PA
and simultaneously in Canada

ISBN 0 285 63354 6

Photoset by Rowland Phototypesetting Ltd
Bury St Edmunds, Suffolk
Printed in Great Britain by
The Guernsey Press Co. Ltd., Guernsey, Channel Islands.

CONTENTS

Foreword

Under the vigilant guidance of Kahlil Gibran we have deserted this world for that inhabited by the occupants of the upper air and set out to compile an anthology of his writings so far unknown to English readers. We have designed a kind of tapestry in which the basic warp and woof consists of Love, its colours subtly modified, sometimes by tears and sometimes by smiles, while the last thread to be woven in is represented by dawn on the day of Death.

This anthology spills out like a rosary of jewelled beads, fashioned originally in the Arabic language and culled from the crucible of our poet-painter's writings: poems in traditional style, prose poems, novels, stories and plays in addition to articles, maxims, correspondence and unpublished manuscripts.

Thus the collection opens with texts that express love and his first youthful visions, followed by essays on visual art and his political pleas for a renaissance of the Middle East; and ending, at maturity, with writings expressing the quintessence of a profound mysticism. If the climax of these visions is the revelation of his own death, Kahlil Gibran remains nonetheless the loving voice that will endure with us as a living presence.

Jean-Pierre Dahdah

The Day I was Born

It was on this very day, twenty-five years ago, that my mother brought me into the world. It was on this very day that silence placed me in the hands of this existence racked with cries and conflict.

Twenty-five times have I orbited the sun, and I know not how many times the moon has gravitated around me. But I have not yet understood the secrets of the light nor penetrated the mysteries of darkness.

Twenty-five times have I gravitated with the moon and the sun, and with the stars, around the supreme Law of the universe. And now my soul murmurs the names of this Law, just as caves echo the waves of the sea; these caves exist only by virtue of the existence of the sea, and yet its existence is unknown to them and, without understanding the sea, they are soothed by the music of its high and low tides.

Twenty-five years ago the hand of time entered my name in the book of this strange and terrible world. And now, like a sibylline word, I symbolise sometimes nothingness and sometimes a host of things.

On this very day, every year, my soul is overwhelmed with thoughts, memories and contemplation. They halt, before my eyes, the procession of days past and show me the spirits of nights gone by; then they disperse them—just as the sun dissolves the fleecy clouds in the sky over the blue horizon—until they vanish into the recesses of my room, just as the songs of the streams die away in the deep and distant valleys.

Each year, on this same day, the spirits that shaped my soul come from the four corners of the world to visit me. They gather round me, intoning the laments of this commemoration; then they withdraw with muffled steps and disappear beyond the invisible world—like flocks of birds which alight in some abandoned courtyard and, after finding no seeds to peck at, flutter about for a few moments, then fly far away to hover in the sky elsewhere.

On this day I see before me the meaning of my past life, as though that life were a little mirror into which I might gaze at length, seeing only the wan faces of the years like the faces of the dead, and the lined features of hopes, dreams and wishes, like the wrinkles of the aged. Then I close my eyes, look into this mirror once more, and see only my own face. I examine it, and I see only sadness; then I question that sadness and find it silent; if it could speak it would be more sublime than the state of blessedness.

During these twenty-five years I have felt so much love. Often I have loved what people hate and destested what they enjoy. I continue today to love what I loved in my youth, and I shall love it until my life's end. Love is all I can possess and no one can deprive me of it.

Many times have I been in love with death; I have invoked it with gentle epithets and adorned it with verses of praise, not only in secret but in the light of day. Although I have not renounced my allegiance to death, I have come to love life. For to me death and life resemble each other in beauty and in pleasure; they unite to nourish my ardour and my nostalgia, while they share between them my passion and my love.

I have loved liberty, and this love grew as I extended my knowledge of the submission of the people to iniquity and ignominy; my love of liberty grew in scope as I learned to understand people's adoration of the hideous idols carved by remote generations, set up in perpetual ignorance and polished by the lips of slaves. And yet I loved these slaves with all my love of liberty and I pitied them, for they are blind men who embrace the jaws of wild beasts without seeing them, swallow the venom of vipers without feeling it and dig their own graves with their fingernails without knowing it.

It is liberty that I have loved most, for I found it

as though I were a young girl who had languished so long in isolation that she had become a transparent shadow among the dwellings, stopping at street corners aned calling out to passers-by who neither turned round nor heeded her.

During those twenty-five years I have, like everyone else, loved happiness; and as each dawn broke, like everyone else, I would go in search of it. But I never found it along their pathways; I found no sign of it even around their palaces, and even less in any echoes emanating from their temples. When I found myself alone in my search for it, I heard my soul whisper these words into my ear: 'Happiness is a vine that takes root and grows within the heart, never outside it.' Then, when I opened the lock-gates of my heart in order to see happiness, I found its mirror, its bed and its clothes, but not happiness itself.

I have loved humanity, I have loved it so much. For me, there are three kinds of men: he who curses life, he who blesses it and he who contemplates it. I loved the first for his wretchedness, the second for his indulgence and the third for his perception.

And so those twenty-five years have gone by, and my days and nights have detached themselves from my life one after the other, like dead leaves whirling in the autumn winds.

Today I pause for a moment for recollection, like that exhausted traveller who halts half-way up the mountain. I look in all directions but can find no trace of my past to which I could point in the light of day and say: 'This is mine.' And I cannot find the harvest of my seasons, apart from the white pages streaked with black ink and strange and random drawings whose lines and colours blend both contrast and harmony. In these writings and sketches I have set my feelings, my thoughts and my dreams, just like the peasant who sows his seeds deep in the earth. After he has finished his work he returns home in the evening, waiting and hoping for the harvest season. But as for me, I have sown the seeds of my heart without expectation or hope.

And now, having reached this stage of my life I see, through a mist of painful sighs, the past rise up, and before me the future appears behind the veil of the past.

Standing in front of my window, I watch existence through the glass and I see people's faces. And I hear their voices rising into space. I observe the rhythm of their steps. I feel the light touch of their spirits and the tides of their desires and the beating of their hearts.

I watch, and I see children playing, running and throwing handfuls of earth at each other, laughing and shouting. I see young men walking with heads held high as though reading the poem of youth at the edges of clouds lined with sunbeams. I see young girls moving like branches swaying in the wind, smiling like flowers as they look at the young men, their eyes thrilling with desire. I see old men walking with cautious steps, their heads bowed with age; gripping their walking-sticks and with their eyes fixed on the ground, as though searching for the pearls they had lost in the time of their youth.

Standing at my window I contemplate these images, and these ghosts who express only noise through their footsteps along the streets and alley-ways of the city. Then I look beyond the city, and I see nature and all it embodies of terrible beauty. And I admire the eloquence of silence, the majesty of the mountains, the humility of the valleys, the vigour of the trees, the waving grasses, the scents of the flowers, the singing of the streams and the rejoicing of the birds.

Then I look beyond nature and I see the sea with all its mysteries hidden in its depths, the ebb and flow of its foaming waves and the great curling shapes rising and falling.

And much further away I see the infinite firma-nent with its floating plants, its gleaming and wandering stars, its suns and satellites, its fixed bodies and all that stands between them, forces of propulsion and attraction that move closer and then further apart, that come to life, then change form—all directed by a law that knows no limit in either time or space.

As I watch through the window I meditate on all these things until I finally forget my twenty-five years, the generations that preceded them and the centuries to come. My existence, with all that I have revealed and hidden concerning it, appears to me like an atom in the sigh of a small child, a moment that trembles in a void stretching from Creation to Eternity.

Yet I feel the existence of this atom, of this soul, of this being that I name 'myself'. I feel its domain and I hear its turmoil. Now it unfolds its wings in the air and stretches its hands in all directions; then it bows down and quivers on this day which, twenty-five years ago, bore witness to its existence. Then a voice of thunder emerges from the sacred depths of its being, crying:

'Peace be with you, O Life. Peace be with you, O Awakening. Peace be with you, O visionary Eye.

Peace be with you, O Day whose brightness floods the darkness of the earth. Peace be with you, O Night that, thanks to your darkness, unveils the fires of the firmament.

Peace be with you, O Seasons. Peace be with you, O Spring that restores youth to the earth. Peace be with you, O Summer that celebrates the glory of the sun. Peace be with you, O Autumn that offers the fruits of effort and the harvest of labour. Peace be with you, O Winter, whose rebellions restore strength to nature.

Peace be with you, O Years that unveil what the years have concealed. Peace be with you, O Generations that purify what generations have sullied. Peace be with you, O Time that leads us towards perfection.

Peace be with you, O Spirit that stands at the

15

helm of life, hiding from us behind the veil of the sun. Peace be with you, O Heart, for you cannot denigrate peace even if you are bathed in tears. Peace be with you, O Lips, for you invoke peace while consumed with bitterness.'

Broken Wings

One day, love, with its magic rays, opened my eyes, and for the first time brushed my soul with its fingers of fire.

I was eighteen years old!

Salma Karamé was the first woman in my life whose charm awakened my spirits and who began to walk before me in that Eden of sublime feelings, when days evaporate like dreams and nights fade out like wedding feasts.

Through her beauty she taught me the cult of the beautiful.

Through her grace she revealed to me the secrets of love.

And through her voice, the first line from the poem of inner life caressed my hearing.

What man does not remember the first girl who through her gentleness and purity transformed the indolence of his youth into an awakening that was fearsome, poignant and devastating?

What man would not be consumed with nostalgia at the memory of that strange moment?

17

Who would refuse to see his being upturned and transformed and his innermost organs expand, spread out and fill with delectable reactions—despite the bitterness induced by modesty—and with pleasurable sensations despite so many tears, desires and nights of insomnia?

In the memory of every man there exists a Salma who appears suddenly in the springtime of his life, infusing his solitude with poetic meaning, filling the emptiness of his days with pleasant company and the silence of his nights with unending melodies.

At that time I was a wanderer between the influences of nature and the inspired interpretation of books and of the Scriptures, when love, through Salma's lips, made itself heard in the ear of my soul.

My life was like a desert, as though paralysed, like the sleep of Adam in paradise, until the day when Salma rose up before me, like a pillar of light.

She became, then, the Eve of that heart filled with mysteries and marvels. It was she who made it grasp the quintessence of existence and set it up like a mirror before the spirits.

That first, headstrong, Eve dragged the acquiescent Adam out of paradise, while Salma Karamé, through her gentleness and the accessibility of my mind, drew me into the Eden of love and purity.

Yet what happened to Adam happened to me.

18

The sword of fire which drove the first man out of paradise was like that sword which terrified me by the brightness of its blade and cast me out of the paradise of love before I broke any commandment, before I tasted the fruit of good and evil.

Today, after all those dark years which removed all trace of the past, this beautiful dream remains in my mind only as painful memories, beating invisible wings around me, drawing anguished sighs from the depths of my being, distilling from my eyes the gall of despair and regret.

Salma the beautiful, the pure, vanished beyond the blue horizon, leaving as her legacy in this world below only the sorrowful moaning of my heart and a marble tomb in the shade of great cypresses.

This tomb and this heart are the only remembrance of Salma Karamé.

Yet this silence that watches over her coffin will not betray the secret concealed by the gods in the darkness of the grave.

And the rustling of those cypress trees, whose roots devour the bodies' elements, will never be able to unveil the mysteries of the tombs.

And the anguish in my heart is expressed now through this black ink, illuminating the phantoms of that tragedy in which the heroes were love, beauty and death.

O friends of my childhood, dispersed throughout the city of Beirut, when you reach that cemetery near the Forest of Pines, enter in silence and walk slowly, lest the sound of your footsteps disturb those who rest in peace, and stop respectfully by Salma's tomb. Greet the earth that embraces her body and invoke my name with a sigh, saying within your heart:

'Here lie buried the hopes of that young man whom the vicissitudes of destiny exiled beyond the seas. Here were his desires entombed and his smile obliterated.

In this silent cemetery his pain grows with the cypresses and the weeping willows. And above this mausoleum his soul hovers every night, reciting funeral verses with the spirits of solitude, mourning with the branches the one who, even yesterday, was a sublime melody on the lips of life and today is no more than a silent secret in the depths of the earth.'

O companions of my youth, in the name of the women you have loved, I entreat you to place a wreath on the grave of the one who was the beloved of my heart.

A flower placed on a forgotten grave is surely like a drop of dew that falls from the eye of dawn on the petals of a shrivelled rose.

For the Love of God, O my Heart

For the love of God, O my heart,
keep the secret of your love
and hide your grief from those around you.
You will reap your reward.
He who reveals his secret has lost his senses.
For silence and mystery mean more
to the one in love.

For the love of God, O my heart,
if anyone asks what befalls you,
do not answer.
And if others inquire:
'Where is she who bewitches you?'
tell them she enchants another heart,
making them think she has slipped from your
    memory.

For the love of God, O my heart,
conceal your longing.
Your suffering and your cure are one.
Reflect on this.

Love in the soul is like wine in the glass:
what you see is the liquid, what is hidden is the
   spirit.

For the love of God, O my heart,
I beg you, hold back your sighs.
Should the heavens fall and the oceans rise,
Feel sure, you shall be saved.

Have Pity, O my Soul

How long will you continue your laments, O my soul, when you know my weakness? How long will you continue to cry out, when I have only human words to describe your dreams?

See, O my soul, I have spent all my life listening to your teachings. Look and wonder, O my tormentor—I have worn out my body in following your footsteps.

My heart once belonged to me, but now it is your slave. My patience kept me company and you have transformed it into a censor. Youth shared my cup and today it blames me. This is all the gods have offered me. What more do you ask and what more are you seeking to covet?

I have denied my being and abandoned the refuge of my life as well as the pride of my days. You are all that remains to me, so judge me fairly—for justice is your glory—or call death down on my body.

Have pity, O my soul! You made me bear a love too great for my heart to contain. You and love are a unified force. As for matter and myself, we are mere crumbs of weakness. Can the struggle between the strong and the weak be delayed?

Have pity, O my soul! You made me see happiness from afar. You and happiness together hold sway on a high mountain, while suffering and I crouch in the bottom of a valley. Can heights and depths ever meet?

Have pity, O my soul! You revealed beauty to me and you concealed it. You and beauty dwell in the light. Ignorance and I survive in the darkness. Can light and dark ever embrace?

You, O soul, enjoy the life beyond before the moment of the Last Judgement, while my body suffers from life while it is still down here.

You walk speedily towards eternity while my body walks unsteadily towards the void. You do not slow, nor does this body hasten. That is the misfortune.

You are drawn up by the pull of heaven and this body is dragged down by the weight of the earth. Neither do you comfort this body, nor does it wish you happiness. That is the horror.

O soul, thanks to your wisdom you are rich and on account of its instinct this body is poor. Neither do you show kindness, nor does the body seek to come to terms. That is the torment.

In the still of the night you will join the beloved and rejoice in her embrace. As for this body, it will

24

remain for ever the victim of discrimination and of the thirst for love. Have pity, O my soul, have pity!

Tear and Smile

My most fervent hope is that my life shall continue as tear and smile: a tear that preserves the purity of my heart and reveals to me the mysteries of life, a smile which brings me closer to the quintessence of my being and symbolises my glorification of the gods; a tear with which I share the misfortunes of all wounded hearts, a smile with which I express my joy in existence.

There is within me a friend who consoles me every time that troubles overwhelm me and misfortunes afflict me. He who does not feel friendship towards himself is a public enemy, and he who finds no confidant within himself will die of despair. For life issues forth from man's inner self and not from what surrounds him.

I have come to say one single word, and I shall say it. But if death were to prevent me from doing so, then it will be said tomorrow. For tomorrow will leave no secret in the book of Eternity.

Letters of Fire

'Here lies one whose name was writ in water.'
John Keats

Is this how nights pass? Is this how they die, trampled beneath the feet of destiny? Is this how generations bury us, retaining nothing of us beyond a name in their journals, written in water instead of ink?

Will this light, this love and these desires wither and vanish? Does death destroy everything we build and does the wind demolish everything we say?

Is life like this? Is it a past that goes by, then crumbles away, and a present that runs in the wake of the past, and a future that can only be grasped if one talks of it in the present or past tense?

Does man dwindle into foam which appears for a moment and, when the breeze blows over it, is then reduced to nothing?

No, I swear it on my life. For the truth of life is life. Neither does it begin deep within the body, nor does it end in a funeral. The years are only a brief moment in a life that goes beyond alpha and omega. Existence on this earth is seen like a dream by the awakening we call the terror of death. It is only a dream, but all that is seen and done then will endure with the existence of God.

The air receives every smile and sigh that issues from our hearts, and retains the echo of every kiss that springs from love. And the angels glean every tear that sadness draws from our eyes, and pass on to the spirits that hover in the limitless universe every melody that joy creates in our hearts.

In the world to come we shall see every wave of our sensations. And we shall reach that quintessance of our divinity that we scorn in our lifetime, driven back as we are by despair.

Distraction, which today we call weakness, will reveal itself tomorrow like a link whose existence is needed for the completion of the chain of human life.

The efforts for which we have not been rewarded will be born again with us and will proclaim our glory. And the misfortunes we endure today will be the laurel wreaths of our tomorrows.

If Keats, that tenor-nightingale, had known that his songs would continue to breathe the love of beauty into the hearts of the living, he would have said: 'Here lies one whose name was writ on the face of heaven in letters of fire.'

One of the First Visions

Over there, in the middle of a field, beside a river of crystalline water, I saw a cage whose sides had been woven by a skilful hand. In one corner was a dead bird and in another two empty saucers, one for water and one for seed.

I stopped, and calm took hold of me. I listened with humility as though that bird and that river were reading me a lesson, interrogating my conscience and questioning my heart. After my meditation I realised that, though so close to a river and to a field, this poor bird must have struggled against hunger and thirst; it must have confronted death while in the cradle of life, like a rich man enclosed in his coffin who must have known hunger and death although surrounded by his gold coins.

A few moments later I suddenly saw the cage change into a transparent human skeleton, and the dead bird became a heart oozing crimson blood; around its wound was the outline of a sorrowing woman's lips.

Then I heard a voice issuing from this wound, saying:

'I am the heart of man, the captive of matter and victim of the laws of mortals. In the field of beauty, beside the river of life, I was imprisoned in the cage of laws made by man for his fellows. Cradled in the beauties of creation and held in the hands of love I died abandoned, for the fruits of those beauties and of that love were forbidden me. According to the customs and rules of mankind, each of my desires was shameful, each of my wishes a humiliation.

'I am the heart of man. I was walled up in the darkness of traditional laws and I wasted away. I was restrained by the fetters of illusion and I was dying. I was abandoned in the far corners of civilisation and I perished. And humanity continues to smile, still tongue-tied and dry-eyed.'

Solitude and Isolation

Life is an island in a sea of solitude and isolation.

For each one of us life is an island where the rocks are our desires and the trees our dreams, where the flowers are our melancholy and the springs our thirst.

Your life, my brother, is an island separate from all other islands and regions. And however many vessels you send to other shores, however many fleets sail to yours, you yourself remain an island isolated within its sorrows and enclosed within its joys, an island remote in its nostalgia, its secrets unknown.

I have seen you, my brother, seated on your little mound of gold, content with your riches and proud of your opulence; you felt that each handful of gold would forge an invisible link between your own thoughts and inclinations and those of other men. You looked to me like a great conqueror, leading your troops to assault fortresses, to destroy and besiege them. But when I looked again, I saw only a solitary wounded heart behind your coffers

31

of gold, like a thirsty bird deprived of water in a gilded cage.

I have seen you, my brother, seated on a glorious throne. All around the people acclaimed you and sang the praises of your virtues and your gifts, their gaze fixed upon you as upon a prophet who with the strength of his soul raises up theirs to the vault of heaven. I have seen you look at them and your face shone with signs of happiness, power and triumph, as if you were for them what the spirit is to the body. But when I looked again I saw your solitary self standing near your throne, suffering in its isolation. Then I saw your self turn to all sides, arms outstretched, as though asking mercy and pity of invisible ghosts; later I saw it look into the distance, over the heads of the crowd, searching for some remote place of shelter which would contain nothing beyond its own solitude.

I have seen you, my brother, very much in love with a beautiful woman, letting your heart melt against her hair and covering her hands with gentle kisses; and I saw her look at you, her eyes sparkling with tenderness and a maternal sweetness imprinted on her lips. I thought then that love had broken your solitude and that you had at last reunited with the universal spirit, who through love draws to himself whatever oblivion has distanced from him. Alas, when I looked again I saw within your captivated heart another, solitary, heart wanting to pour out its secrets to that woman—but in vain. And I saw behind your soul, melting with love, another solitary soul, like a cloud that would have liked to turn into tears in your companion's hand—but in vain.

Your life, my brother, is a lonely house, far from all dwellings and all settlements.

Your inner life is a house far from the paths leading to appearance that men denote by your name. If that house were dark, you could not light it with your neighbour's lamp; nor, if it were empty, could you fill it with his riches. If it stood in a desert, you could not transport it into a garden worked by other hands; and if it perched on top of a mountain you could not bring it down into a valley trodden by other feet.

Your inner life, my brother, is girdled by solitude and isolation. And without that solitude and that isolation you would not be what you are, neither would I be what I am. Without that isolation and that solitude I could believe, when I hear your voice, that it is my voice that is speaking; and that when I see your face, I see the reflection of my own face in a mirror.

The Mother

For every being on earth the most limpid word is that of 'mother' and the sweetest call is that of 'mummy'. These few letters with their sublime meaning are moulded in hope and love and everything that is fine and pure in the heart of man.

The mother is everything in life. She is the consolation in our sadness, the help in our distress, the strength in our weakness. She is the source of tenderness, compassion and forgiveness.

He who loses his mother loses a breast on which to lay his head, a hand that blesses him and a gaze that protects him.

The Woman of Tomorrow

Marriage in our time is a business as comical as it is dramatic. It is controlled by the young men as well as by the fathers of the girls. The suitors win in most cases, whereas the fathers-in-law always lose. As for the girls, they pass like merchandise from one house to the other. As the days go by they lose their *joie de vivre* and, like old furniture, they will be abandoned in the far corners of the houses, condemned to a slow decay.

It is true that today's civilisation has to a small extent developed women's education, but on the other hand it has increased their suffering by leaving the field open to all the desires of man.

In the past woman was a happy servant; today she is an unhappy Lady. Whereas she once walked blindly in the light of day, she now walks with her eyes wide open in the darkness.

She was beautiful in her ignorance, virtuous in her simplicity and strong in her very weakness. She has become ugly through her artifice, superficial in her senses, heartless through her knowledge.

Will the day come when beauty and understanding, artifice and virtue, weakness of body and strength of soul will be united within woman?

The Sister Soul

I think that human society became corrupt when man encountered the half that is different from himself and woman remained with the half that is divergent from herself. And I think that a corrupt marriage often produces rotten fruit. Criminals, wrong-doers, the wretched and the lazy are born of the spiritual loathing between husband and wife.

I want to see no more families living in poverty, hatred and unhappiness. If I could destroy all the homes built upon hypocrisy, lies and deceit, I should not hesitate for a moment. Do you know among your friends a husband or wife who could honestly say to you that they are living with the true half—the one that came forth, their hand in the other's, in a single flash from the bosom of God?

In Europe today sociologists try to find ways of increasing the birth rate, without regard to the homes where this birth rate has its origins. They care little whether the child comes from the light of life or the darkness of repugnance; the important thing for them is that the child should exist. I see this as pure ignorance. For a nation consisting of a million fine and enlightened souls is far better than one of a hundred million souls that are depraved and idle.

The Man on the Cross

Every year on this very day [Good Friday] humanity wakes with a start from its deep sleep. It stands
before the spirits of past generations and gazes,
eyes brimming with tears, towards the Hill of
Calvary, remembering Jesus of Nazareth who was
crucified there. And when the sun sinks behind the
margin of the day, humanity gathers before the
statues erected on the summit of each hill and at
the foot of each mountain.

On that day the commemoration brings Christian spirits from all over the world to converge on
Jerusalem. They flock there, beating their breasts
as they contemplate a spirit wearing a crown of
thorns, holding out his arms towards the infinite
and gazing through the veil of death into the
depths of life. And barely has night lowered the
curtain on the theatre of this day's events than
the Christians collapse in groups, in the shadow of
forgetfulness, between the sheets of ignorance and
indolence.

On this day, every year, the philosophers leave

their dark lairs, the thinkers their cold hermitages and the poets their imaginary valleys. All stand in deferential silence, listening to the voice of a young man who says of these criminals: 'Father, forgive them, for they know not what they do.' But as soon as silence obscures the voices of light, the philosophers, thinkers and poets turn back and bury their souls in their outmoded books.

On this day, women devoted to *joie de vivre* and to finery and dress leave their houses to go and see the mourning mother who stands before the cross, like a tender sapling in a raging storm. As they approach her they hear her deep groans and grief-stricken sobs.

As for the young men who run with the rapid passing of the days towards a destination unknown to them, they stop for a moment to see the young Mary Magdalen wash with her tears the blood-stained feet of a man who hangs between heaven and earth. And when they tire of this scene they run away laughing.

Every year on this day, humanity wakes with the spring and weeps for the sufferings of Jesus of Nazareth. Then they close their eyes and fall into a deep sleep. But spring remains awake, smiling and advancing until the moment when it merges into summer, the season clad in a golden garment full of fragrance.

Humanity is a [weeping] woman who takes pleasure in lamenting over the heroes of past centuries. But if humanity were a [more virile] man it would rejoice in the glory of its heroes. Humanity is like a child weeping over a dying bird. Yet it is afraid to confront a terrible storm that snaps off dead branches and blows the remains far away.

Humanity sees in Jesus of Nazareth a man who was born poor, who lived like a wretch and was humiliated like a weakling, crucified as a criminal. And humanity honours him only with funeral orations, lamentations and weeping.

For nineteen centuries human beings have worshipped mildness in the person of Jesus—whereas Jesus was strong, but people have no understanding of his true strength.

Jesus did not live in poverty or in fear; neither did he die suffering or complaining. But he lived in revolt, was crucified as a rebel and died a giant.

Jesus was not a bird with broken wings—he was a raging storm whose breath shattered every crooked wing.

Jesus did not come from beyond the blue horizon in order to make suffering a symbol of life, but rather to make of life a symbol of truth and liberty.

Jesus feared neither his enemies nor his persecutors, nor did he lament in the face of his executioners. But he expressed his message freely in public, boldly confronting oppression and tyranny. When he saw hideous pustules, he would lance them. If he heard evil talk he would stifle it. And when he encountered hypocrisy he would strike it down.

Jesus did not come down from the supreme circle of light to destroy dwellings and build church steeples and monasteries over their ruins, nor to persuade men to become priests or pastors. He came to breathe into the air of this earth a spirit as powerful as it was new, with the strength to undermine the foundations of all the monarchies erected over the bones of mankind; he came to demolish the palaces constructed over the tombs of the weak and to destroy the idols erected over the corpses of the poor.

Jesus did not come to teach men how to build huge cathedrals and opulent temples alongside humble cottages and cold, dark hovels. He came to make the heart of man into a temple, his soul into an altar, and his spirit into a priest.

Such was the mission of Jesus of Nazareth and such were the principles for which he was ready to be crucified. And if people were wise, they would stand up on this day and sing joyful hymns of victory.

O sublime victim of crucifixion, you who from the summit of Golgotha see the processions of generations, you who hear the din of nations and understand the dreams of eternity, you are more majestic, more venerable on the bloodstained cross than a thousand kings on a thousand thrones in a thousand kingdoms. And, moreover, poised between your mortal agony and death itself you are more fearsome than a thousand generals at the head of a thousand soldiers in a thousand battles.

But with all your sorrow, you are more joyful than flowers in springtime. With all your suffering, you remain more serene than the angels in their heaven. In the face of those who flagellate you, you are freer than sunlight.

Your crown of thorns is more sublime than Bahram's crown. The nail that pierces your hand is nobler than Jupiter's sceptre. The bloodstains on your feet are more resplendent than Astarte's jewels.

Forgive these poor creatures who weep over you today, for they know not how to lament over their own fate. Forgive them, for they know not that you have conquered death through death and that you have given life to those who lie in their tombs.

Kahlil the Ungodly

Do you know, O weak and docile ones, the nature of this priest who frightens you, he whom you have set up as guardian of your souls' most sacred secrets? Listen to me: I shall explain to you what you feel yourselves and fear to bring out into the open.

He is a traitor. The Christians give him a holy book and he turns it into a device for capturing their possessions. He is a hypocrite: he carries a fine cross given to him by the faithful which he makes into a sharp-edged sword, holding it over their heads. He is a tyrant: when the weak offer him their necks, he bridles and shackles them, restraining them with an iron hand and letting them go only after shattering them like earthen pots and scattering the fragments like ashes.

He is a ferocious wolf who gets into the sheep-fold. The shepherd mistakes him for a sheep and quietly goes off to sleep; and under cover of darkness the wolf pounces on the ewes and slays them one by one.

He is a glutton, showing more respect for well laden tables than for the altars in the temple. He is rapacious, pursuing the dinar right into the caves of the jinn. He sucks the blood of mortals as the sand of the desert absorbs drops of rain. He is a grasping miser who saves what he does not need.

He is a trickster who enters through the cracks in the walls and leaves only when the house falls down. He is a thief with a heart of stone who snatches the widow's mite and the orphan's farthing.

He is a strange being, with the beak of an eagle, the claws of a leopard and the teeth of a hyena, and he moves like a viper. Take away from him his book, rend his vestments, pull out the hairs from his beard—do with him what you will—then place a dinar in his hand and he will forgive you with a loving smile. Strike his cheek, spit in his face, stamp on his neck; then invite him to your table, and he will cheerfully forget everything as he loosens his belt to let his stomach swell with your food and drink. Blaspheme his God, ridicule his beliefs, laugh at his faith; then offer him a jar of wine or a basket of fruit, and he will forgive you and find excuses for you before God and men.

When he sees a woman he looks away and cries as loudly as he can: 'Get thee behind me, daughter of Babel.' Then he says to himself: 'It is better to marry than to burn.' When he sees a crowd of amorous adolescents he raises his eyes to heaven and cries: 'Vanity of vanities, all is vanity under the sun.' Then he goes off on his own with a sigh and says: 'May those laws be abolished, may those traditions perish which have deprived me of life's blessings and denied me the pleasures of existence.'

He tells people: 'Judge not, lest ye be judged.' But he judges very severely all those who laugh at his threats, and condemns them to hell even before their life is over. As he speaks to you he looks at the sky from time to time, but his thought, like a viper, constantly slithers towards your pockets. He addresses you, saying: 'My children, my sons', without feeling the merest paternal affection, knowing neither how to smile at a newborn baby nor how to take a child on his knee. He tells you, with a pious shake of his head: 'Let us rise above the things of this world, for our lives disperse like mist and our days fade away like shadows.' But if you observe him carefully you will see how he holds on to the coat-tails of life, regretting yesterday, frightened by the rapid passing of today and pursuing tomorrow.

He asks you for charity, although he is richer than you. If you give him alms he blesses you openly, and if you give him nothing he curses you in secret. In church he commends you to help the poor and needy while hungry people cry out around his house, and when the wretched hold out their hands before his eyes he neither sees nor hears. At his altar he sells his prayer; he who does not buy it will be considered unfaithful to God and to his prophets and will be deprived of paradise and eternal life.

There, O Christians, is the creature who frightens you. There, O poor creatures, is the monk who sucks your blood. This is the priest who with his right hand makes the sign of the cross and with his left grabs hold of your hearts. This is the bishop whom you choose to serve you but who becomes your master, the man whom you canonise as a saint but who turns into a demon, the man whom you elevate to the dignity of representative but who becomes a heavy burden.

Mad John

Look, O Jesus of Nazareth, from where you sit, deep within the circle of sublime light. Look across the blue vault at this earth of whose elements the garment you wore yesterday was made. Look, O faithful guardian—the wild thorns have stifled the flowers whose seeds you watered with the sweat of your brow. Look, O good shepherd— the claws of wild beasts have torn the flanks of the feeble lamb you carried on your shoulders. Look, your noble blood has seeped into the bowels of the earth, your hot tears have dried in the hearts of men, your warm breath has been blown away by the winds of the desert, the field that your feet once sanctified has become a battlefield where the boots of the strong crush the flanks of the fallen, where the hands of tyrants snatch life from the weak.

The cries of the poor and the moans of the wretched that rise from the darkness are heard neither by those who reign in your name, nor by those who speak of your teachings from the heights of the pulpit. The sheep that you sent for the word of life have changed into wild beasts whose teeth tear the wings from the sheep that you clasped in your arms. And the word of life that you brought down from the bosom of God has disappeared into books and been replaced by a fearful tumult that makes souls quake with terror.

O Jesus, they have built churches and temples to the glory of their own names, they have decked them out in woven silk and molten gold, and left the bodies of your chosen poor lying naked in the cold streets; they have filled space with the smoke of incense and the flames of candles; they have let those who believe in your divinity know hunger and cry famine; they have laden the air with praise and hymns, while hearing neither the appeals of the orphans nor the widows' sighs.

Come a second time, O living Jesus, and drive these merchants of religion out of your temples, of which they have made dens crawling with the vipers of their tricks and lies. Come and ask these Caesars to account for themselves – they have taken from the weak what belongs to them and what belongs to God. Come and see the vine you planted with your right hand: worms have eaten the stocks and the feet of vagabonds have destroyed the grapes. Come and see those to whom you entrusted peace—they grew disunited, became enemies and fought each other; all that remains of their warring strife are our grieving souls and our heavy hearts.

In their festivals and ceremonies they boldly

raise their voices, saying: 'Glory be to God in the highest, on earth peace, and joy to mankind.' Does God, your heavenly father, glorify Himself when He hears His name pronounced by lying tongues and by the lips of criminals? Is there peace on earth when the wretched in the fields sap their strength in the heat of the sun in order to feed the strong and fill the bellies of tyrants? Is there any joy among mankind when the wretched look on death with longing, as the vanquished warrior looks on his saviour?

Slavery

Men are the slaves of life; and it is slavery that fills their days with scorn and shame, drowning their nights in blood and tears.

Seven thousand years have passed since my first birth, and thus far I have seen only submissive slaves and prisoners in chains.

I have scoured the countries of East and West, I have traversed the light and shade of life; I have seen nations and peoples walking in procession from caves to skyscrapers. Yet so far I have seen only shoulders bowed beneath the weight of yokes, arms in fetters and knees bent before idols.

I have followed man from Babel to Paris, from Nineveh to New York; I have seen on the sand traces of the chains that followed his footprints, and I have heard the moans of generations and of centuries echoing from the valleys and the forests.

I have entered castles, institutes and temples and halted at the foot of thrones, altars and pulpits; there I have seen the worker enslaved to the trader, the trader enslaved to the soldier, the soldier enslaved to the governor, the governor enslaved to the king, the king enslaved to the priest, the priest enslaved to the idol—and the idol was nothing more than mud moulded by demons and erected on a pile of skulls.

I have entered the dwellings of the rich and powerful as well as the hovels of the poor and weak, and I have paused in alcoves adorned with ivory carvings and gold plating as well as in lairs haunted by the ghosts of despair and by the smell of death; there I saw newborn babies absorb slavery along with their mothers' milk, I saw boys learning submission along with the letters of the alphabet, I saw young girls dressing in garments lined with servility and women collapse on beds of serfdom.

I have followed generations from the banks of the Ganges to the great buildings of London by way of the banks of the Euphrates, the Nile delta, Mount Sinai, the market-places of Athens, the alleyways of Constantinople and the churches of Rome. Everywhere, in processions before the altars, I saw slavery advancing, and I heard the generations naming it god; they poured wines and perfumes over its feet and named it king; they burned incense before its statues and named it prophet; they prostrated themselves before it and named it law; they fought and killed each other for it and named it patriotism; they submitted to its will and named it the shadow of God on earth; they burned down their own homes and demolished their own edifices in obedience to its will, calling it fraternity and equality; then they laboured and fought for it, calling it commerce and money.

Thus slavery has many names but only one reality, numerous guises but only one essence. Moreover, slavery is an eternal evil, with neither beginning nor end, manifesting itself in different symptoms and impairments that children inherit from their parents, just as they inherit the breath of life; and the centuries cast its seeds into the soil of centuries, just as the seasons harvest what is sown by the seasons.

Here are the strangest forms of slavery that I have encountered:

Blind slavery is that which binds people's present life to their parents' past, which makes their souls bow down before the traditions of their ancestors and gives them new bodies in place of old spirits, repainted tombs in place of dry bones.

Dumb slavery is that which ties a man's life to the skirts of a woman he hates, clamps a wife's body to the bed of the husband she detests and stitches their two lives into one, like a single shoe.

Deaf slavery is that which forces the individual to follow the same leanings as his particular circle, to wear the same colours and the same clothes, becoming in this way an echo without a voice, a shadow without a body.

Limping slavery is that which puts vigorous men under the yoke of the cunning, and makes them submit their strength to those who are greedy for honour and glory; in this way they are manipulated like puppets, only to be discarded tomorrow.

Hideous slavery is that which brings the souls of the newborn down from the wide firmament into wretched homes where poverty and ignorance, dishonour and despair, live side by side; they will grow into unhappy people, then into malefactors, and will end as outcasts.

Chameleon-like slavery is that which buys things at an unfair price and endows values with names that are not theirs; it describes verbiage as knowledge, spite as intelligence, weakness as kindness and cowardice as pride.

Underhand slavery is that which uses fear to loosen the tongues of the weak: in the end they speak of things that they do not feel and express ideas that are in no way their inmost beliefs, becoming in this way like pieces of cloth that are ironed and hung up.

Hunchbacked slavery is that which leads one people according to the laws of another.

Leprous slavery is that which, as soon as the king is dead, places his son on the throne.

Black slavery is that which brands the innocent sons of criminals with shame.

And, finally, slavery for slavery's sake, which is the power to perpetuate itself.

When I was tired of pursuing the generations and

weary of looking at processions of people and of nations, I sought solitary rest in the valley of ghosts, where the shadows of times past hide and the spirits of the future fall into a half-sleep. There I saw a fleshless spectre walking alone and looking directly at the sun. I asked him:

'Who are you?'

'I am liberty.'

'But where are your sons, then?'

'One died on the cross, another died mad and the third is not yet born.'

Then he vanished from my eyes into the mist.

My People are Dead

My people are dying while I, who am still alive, weep for them in my solitude.

My people are about to die and the valleys of my country run with tears and blood.

Some have been cut down by the sword and others by hunger, while I am in this distant land, among people who sleep happily in their comfortable beds. And a terrible tragedy takes hold in the depths of my soul.

Alas, I am neither an ear of corn in the fields of Syria nor a ripe fruit in the valleys of Lebanon. And this is truly the misfortune that makes me deserving of scorn, both my own and that of the spectres of the night.

My people are dying on the cross, their hands stretched out towards both East and West, their eyes fixed on the darkness of the firmament.

They are dying in silence; for humanity, weary of their cries, has stopped its ears.

They are dying of hunger in the land that once overflowed with milk and honey.

They are dying because the vipers and the offspring of vipers have poured their poison into the air that once knew the scent of cedars and the fragrance of roses and jasmine.

What can we do for those who are still in their death throes?

Our lamentations will not satisfy their hunger, neither will our tears quench their thirst.

O my Syrian brothers, the feeling that prompts you to give a fragment of your life to someone in danger of losing his is the only virtue that makes you worthy of the light of day and of the peace of the night.

The coin that you might give to those who hold out their hands to us is the one golden link that unites the human within you to the superhuman.

Sleeping Draughts

The Levantines live in the theatres of centuries gone by; they tend towards a negative attitude as distracting as it is amusing; they detest both positive and abstract principles as well as positive and abstract teachings, which irritate them, waking them from a deep sleep.

That is how day follows night, while the Levantine remains slumped on his soft bed; he wakes for a moment when the fleas bite, then, thanks to narcotics which mingle in his blood and circulate through his veins he drowses for a whole generation. If one man stands up, summons the sleepers and fills their dwellings, temples and tribunals with turmoil the Levantines will open eyes heavy with eternal sleep and say with a yawn: 'What a lout! He can't sleep and won't let anyone else do so.' Then they close their eyes again and murmur into the listening ears of their minds: 'He is a miscreant, an atheist who is trying to corrupt the morals of youth and destroy the structures of past generations.'

If people want me to transform my lamentations into laughter, my repugnance into sympathy and my extremism into moderation, then let them show me among the Levantines a fair-minded ruler, an honest legislator, a religious leader who behaves in accordance with what he has learnt, a husband who when he looks at his wife sees in her his own soul.

You and Us

We are the sons of grief and you are the sons of rejoicing. We are the sons of grief, and grief is a divine shadow which does not dwell near evil hearts. Our souls are steeped in sadness, and the sadness is so deep that shallow souls cannot contain it. We weep and we moan, O you who mock. He who washes himself once with his tears will remain pure until the end of time.

You erected pyramids with the skulls of slaves and now the pyramids stand in the sand, speaking to the generations of our immortality and your ruin. We destroyed the Bastille with the arms of liberators, and the Bastille became an example followed by other nations, blessing us and cursing you. You crucified Jesus of Nazareth and mocked him to his face, yet one hour later he came down from the cross and walked like a giant, conquering the generations with his spirit and his truth, filling the earth with his glory and his beauty. You poisoned Socrates, stoned Paul, killed Galileo, assassinated Ali ibn Abu Talib [the father of

Shiism] and strangled Midhat Pasha [leader of the Young Turkey party]; but, like victorious heroes standing before eternity, they are still alive.

And you, you live in the memory of mankind like corpses lying on the ground, with nobody to bury them in the darkness of oblivion and nothingness. We are the sons of grief, and grief is like rain that falls full of goodness and knowledge. You are the sons of rejoicing and, however loud your laughter, it will remain like columns of smoke demolished by the wind and the elements.

O Sons of my Mother

What do you ask of me, sons of my Mother? I have sung for you and nobody wanted to dance. I have uttered lamentations before you and nobody wanted to weep. Do you want me to sing and weep at the same time?

I loved you, sons of my Mother; and love did me damage, and was no use to you. Today I hate you, for hate is a torrent that carries away only dead branches and destroys only those houses that are threatened with ruin.

I felt compassion for your weakness, sons of my Mother, but compassion multiplies the weak as well as the idle, and does not profit life in any way. And now I have only to see your weakness for my soul to shudder in disgust and recoil in disdain.

What do you ask of me, then, sons of my Mother—or rather, what do you hope for from life when life no longer counts you among its sons?

In the grip of priests and charlatans, your souls tremble; caught in the teeth of bloodsuckers and tyrants, your bodies shudder; and your nation trembles beneath the boots of the conquering enemy. Your swords are rusty, your spears broken and your shields pierced. Why, then, do you remain on the field of battle?

Your religion is hypocrisy, your life is boastfulness—so what can be your fate, if not to turn to dust? Why, then, are you alive since death is the sleep of the wretched?

I hate you, sons of my Mother, for you hate glory and nobility. I scorn you, for you scorn yourselves. I am your enemy because you are the enemies of the gods. But you do not know it.

Open Letter from a Christian Poet to the Moslems

I am Lebanese and proud to be so. I am not Turkish, and I am proud not to be.

I belong to a nation whose splendours I praise, but there is no state to which I might belong or where I might find refuge.

I am a Christian and proud to be so. But I love the Arab prophet and I appeal to the greatness of his name; I cherish the glory of Islam and fear lest it decay.

I am a Levantine, and although in exile I remain Levantine by temperament, Syrian by inclination and Lebanese by feeling.

I am oriental, and the Orient has an ancient civilisation of magical beauty and of fragrant and exquisite taste. Although I admire the present state of Western civilisation and the high degree of development and progress it has attained, the East will remain the country of my dreams and the setting for my desires and longings.

In the regions that stretch from the heart of India to the Maghreb and from the Persian Gulf to the Caucasian mountains, in those countries that have engendered kings and prophets, heroes and poets—in those sacred lands my soul freely wanders, repeating the songs of past glory and scanning the horizon where a new glory is taking shape.

Some of you treat me as a renegade, for I hate the Ottoman state and hope it will disappear. To those amongst you Gibran answers: 'I hate the Ottoman state, for I love Islam, and I hope that Islam will once again find its splendour.'

I love the Koran and I despise those who use it to prevent any Moslem rising [against the Turkish government], just as I disdain those who manipulate Christians in the name of the Gospel.

What is it in the Ottoman state that so attracts you, since it has destroyed the edifices of your glory? Is it not death that covets your existence? Did Islamic civilisation not die with the start of the Ottoman conquests? Have the Arabian princes not suffered a decline since the advance of the Mongol sultans? Has the green flag not been hidden in the fog since the red flag appeared over a mass of skulls?

As a Christian, as one who has harboured Jesus in one half of his heart and Mohammed in the other, I promise you that if Islam does not succeed in defeating the Ottoman state the nations of Europe will dominate Islam. If no one among you rises up against the enemy within, before the end of this generation the Levant will be in the hands of those whose skins are white and whose eyes are blue.

Words and Thoughts

Is not a weak woman the symbol of a subject nation? Does not a woman torn apart by the inclinations of her soul and by her body's fetters resemble a nation overwhelmed by its leaders and its clergy? Woman is to the nation what light is to a lamp. If the oil were lacking, would not the lamp lose its glow?

*   *   *

Listen to a woman when she looks at you, not when she speaks to you.

*   *   *

The day will come when someone will say: 'In remote antiquity men married, went to war and chased after gold.' To which another will reply: 'Those are traditions to which History does not bear witness.'

*   *   *

I owe woman my whole life, I owe her this self that

was born of a cry, I owe her all my writings. Woman opened my eyes, freed my soul. Without woman-mother, woman-sister and woman-friend I would have slept like all those who, in the bliss of this world, sleep and snore.

*   *   *

In future, when you see something and want not to take it but to abandon yourself to it, tell yourself that this thing is Beauty.

*   *   *

When you complain to your neighbour about some misfortune, you are offering him part of your heart. If his soul is noble, he will be grateful to you; if his soul is base, he will despise you.

*   *   *

The earth is my country, humanity, my family.

*   *   *

I love you, my brother, whoever you are. I love you as you pray in the mosque, as you practise your devotions in church or worship in your temple. For you and I are the children of one single religion: the Spirit. The various pathways of this religion represent the different fingers of the single loving hand of the Supreme Being. And, to guide us towards the fulfilment of the Soul, this hand stretches out towards us with ardour.

*　　*　　*

Humility is a veil that conceals the features of greatness, while vanity is a mask that disguises the face of misfortune.

*　　*　　*

I have never expressed hate except as a means of defending myself. Had I been stronger, I would not have had to resort to such a weapon.

*　　*　　*

The heart, with all the various feelings that branch off from it, is like a cedar tree. If it should lose a main branch it will certainly suffer, but it will not die. Rather, it will channel all its vitality into the branch next to it, allowing the new growth to fill the place left by the branch that was cut away.

*　　*　　*

The earth breathes in and we utter our first cry. The earth breathes out, and we utter our last sigh.

*　　*　　*

Even if the mill-wheel were to break, the river would pursue its course towards the sea.

*　　*　　*

Life knows nothing of chance. In the universe there are innumerable threads that make up the canvas of the primary universe. Your life and mine are just two threads in this eternal canvas. They diverge, converge and interweave with each other, then diverge and converge again until the fabric is complete. The Weaver who sits behind His loom knows where each thread goes. But no thread knows the Weaver's plan. Everything has a mission; once that mission is accomplished, its author departs.

*　　　*　　　*

Life consists of debts and credits. One day it gives and the next day it makes demands; then it gives again, then makes more demands, and so forth until this ebb and flow of exchanges wears us out. And in the end we shall abandon ourselves to the sublime sleep.

*　　　*　　　*

Most religions speak of God in the masculine. As I see him, he is as much a mother as a father. He is father and mother at the same time. And woman is the example of the maternal God. We can grasp the paternal God through reason or imagination, but to meet with the maternal God we must go by way of the heart, through love.

*　　　*　　　*

In reincarnation I have found the key to life and death, like a lantern illuminating the subterranean passageways in people's relationships with one another.

Imagine how many steps we have taken before

meeting each other. And each step was the consequence of the previous step and the cause of the one that followed.

The cycle of life is not ended by one life or by several. We aspire to perfection. We are searching for God. And who can find God in twenty years, in a hundred years or in a thousand?

*　　*　　*

Knowledge causes its own seeds to grow, but it could not sow seeds within you.

*　　*　　*

A truth which needs to be proved is a half-truth.

*　　*　　*

Get behind me, wisdom that does not weep, philosophy that does not laugh, greatness that does not bow before children.

*　　*　　*

At low tide I wrote a sentence in the sand expressing all my soul and all my spirit.

At high tide I went back to re-read and reflect on what I had written, but all along the shore I found only my own ignorance.

*　　*　　*

He who does not spend his time in the kingdom of dreams is a slave to his own days.

O Earth

How beautiful you are, Earth, and how resplendent!

How total is your obedience to the light and how noble your submission to the sun!

How graceful you are when cloaked in shadow, and how seductive is your face beneath the mask of darkness!

How melodious are your dawn songs and how magnificent your rejoicings at dusk!

How perfect you are, Earth, and how sublime!

I have wandered your plains and climbed your mountains; I have gone down to your valleys and into your caves. Thus I have known your dreams on the plain, your pride on the mountain, your peace in the valley, your firmness in the rock, your silence in the cave. You are relaxed in their strength, haughty in their modesty, humble in their arrogance, gentle in their resistance, lucid in their secrets.

I have sailed your seas, crossed your rivers and

walked along your river banks. I have heard eternity speak through your ebb and flow, I have heard the ages sing their hymns across your hills and dales, I have heard life whisper to itself in your mountain passes and along their slopes. You are the tongue and the lips of eternity, the cords and fingers of time, the thoughts of life and its proclamation.

Your spring awoke me and led me towards your forests, where your sighs rise up in spirals of incense. Your summer urged me to sit down in your fields, where your labour brings forth fruit. Your autumn invited me to meditate over your vineyards, where your blood runs in the guise of wine. Your winter took me into its bed where your purity scatters its snowflakes. You are fragrance in their springtime and generosity in their summer; in their autumn you are bountiful, and in their winter crystal-clear.

One starry night I opened the lock-gates of my soul and went out to meet you, dragging with me the chains of my cupidity and selfishness. And I saw you looking at the stars, and they smiled back at you. Then I cast off my chains and discovered that your universe is where the soul dwells, that its desires and its harmony dwell within yours, and that its joy lies in those golden sequins that the firmament scatters over your body.

One stormy night, weary of my idle dreaming and inertia, I went to meet you. And you appeared to me like a fearsome giant, armed with tempests, fighting your past by means of your present, pursuing and destroying what was old and weak within you with the aid of what was new and strong within you. In this way I learned that the laws and rules of conduct are yours, as are the deeds and gestures of man. I learned that he who by dint of his own tempest does not break his dead branches will die of ennui, that he who by dint of his own tempests does not shed his dead leaves will die of indolence, and that he who does not bury in oblivion whatever is dead within his past will himself be a shroud for what follows.

O Earth, how generous you are and how persevering!

How great is your tenderness for your children, who turn away from their truths to give themselves over to their illusions; who are lost between what they have gained and what they lack in order to progress further!

We cry out, and you smile.

We kill, and you pay the penalty.

We blaspheme, and you bless.

We sully, and you sanctify.

We sleep without dreaming, and you dream in your eternal wakefulness.

We pierce your breast with swords and lances, and you heal our wounds with ointment and balm.

We sow in your hands bones and skulls, from which you bring forth poplars and willows.

We store carrion deep within you, and you fill our threshing floors with armfuls of wheat and our wine-presses with grapes.

We smear your face with blood, and you wash ours with nectar.

We exploit your elements in order to make cannon and rockets, and you use ours to make roses and lilies grow.

O Earth, how vast is your forbearance, how vast your magnanimity!

What are you, Earth, and who are you?

Are you that speck of dust raised by the feet of God on His way from the east of the universe to the west, or that spark fired from the hearth of infinity?

Are you that seed tossed into the field of the upper air, destined, by the will of its flesh, to burst from its husk and become a divine tree reaching up beyond the atmosphere?

Are you that drop of blood in the veins of the Titan among giants, or that bead of sweat on his forehead?

Are you that fruit serenely ripening in the sun? Or the fruit on the tree of universal knowledge whose roots reach down into the depths of alpha and whose branches rise to the heights of omega? Or else that jewel placed by the god of time in the palm of the goddess of space?

Are you that child in the arms of the universe? Or that old woman who, although replete with their wisdom, examines the days and the nights?

What are you, Earth, and who are you?

You are me, O Earth! You are my sight and my perception. You are my reflections and my imaginings as well as my dreams. You are my hunger and my thirst, my sorrow and my joy, my heedlessness and my vigilance.

You are the beauty in my eyes, the ardent desire in my heart, the immortality in my soul.

You are me, O Earth! For if I did not exist, you would not be there!

Paris

Happy are those with a haven in Paris. Happy are those who walk along the banks of the Seine, browsing over old books and prints. In this town [Boston] full of friends and acquaintances, I feel myself exiled at the end of the world where life is as cold as the snow, as dull as ashes, as silent as the sphinx.

Paris, Paris, theatre of the arts and of thought, source of imagination and of dreams! In Paris I was born a second time, and in Paris I should like to spend the rest of my life; but I want my grave to be in Lebanon. If destiny smiles on me and realises some of the dreams that today flutter through my mind, I shall return to Paris to appease my starving heart and quench my soul's thirst. I shall return there to eat its divine bread and drink its magical wine.

Art

Some believe that art is the imitation of nature; in fact, nature is so sublime that it cannot be imitated. However noble it may be, art cannot perform a single one of the miracles of nature. And besides, why imitate nature when it can be perceived by all those endowed with senses?

Art consists, rather, of understanding nature and transmitting our understanding to those who are unaware of it. The mission of art is to communicate the spirit of the tree, not to draw a trunk, branches and leaves which look like a tree. The aim of art is to reveal the consciousness of the sea, not to paint foaming waves or azure water.

Life is naked. And a naked body represents the closest and finest symbol of life. If I draw a mountain as a heap of human shapes, or if I paint a waterfall made up of naked bodies in downward flow, it is because I see in a mountain a mass of living things and in a waterfall a rushing stream of life.

Art is a sublime divinity, the hem of whose gown can be touched only with fingers purified by fire, and of whose face nothing can be seen beyond eyelids bathed in tears.

Music

I sat down close to her who was the beloved of my soul and listened to what she said. I was all ears and said not a word, and I felt in her voice a strength which electrified my heart and parted me from my being. Then my soul began to float in a space that knew no limit. Might the universe be a dream and the body a cage?

A strange magic entered my beloved's voice and my feelings were seduced by it. I began to take less heed of her words than of what took their place.

It was music, my friends. I heard it whenever my beloved sighed after certain words and smiled after others. I heard it when she uttered words that were broken off or that ran together, and yet others that hung half-spoken on her lips.

As though my hearing had eyes, I perceived the emotions within her heart, I withdrew from the essence of her words to move closer to the jewels that were her feelings—which materialised in a music that is the voice of the soul.

Music is truly the language of souls, and melodies are the balmy breezes that play on the heart-strings. They are fairy fingers that tap lightly on the door of the feelings and awaken memories buried in the depths of the past.

It is the quivering of a string, charged with waves from the upper air, which penetrates your hearing, then emerges from your eyes in a burning tear provoked by tender thoughts of a distant love or by the painful blows of destiny. And these notes may surface on your lips in a smile of fulfilment.

Music's body is one last sigh; its soul is breath; its spirit, heart.

And in the words of a Persian poet: 'Music is a houri in the paradise of the gods who was in love with an Earthling. When she came down to tell him of her love, the gods, in a fury, ordered a terrible wind to pursue her. Scattering her through the air, it dispersed her to all the corners of the earth. But she did not die, and lives still in the ears of mortals.'

Music is the echo of the first kiss bestowed by Adam on the lips of Eve. And ever since, this echo has made pleasure rebound on to fingers as they play and on ears as they listen.

Let us pay homage to all the great musicians who have taught men to see with their ears and hear with their hearts.

Give me the Nay*

What is life, if not a sleep charmed
by the dreams of him who achieves the will of
   the soul.
Secrecy in the soul is masked by its very sadness;
if this were to vanish, secrecy would wear the
   mask of joy.
And secrecy in life is veiled by the very riches of
   life.
If this veil were lifted, the veil of wretchedness
   would take its place.
So if you value yourself beyond riches and
   beyond wretchedness,

*The nay is the enchanted flute of the Sufis, but also the syrinx
played by the Greek god Pan. It expresses the harmony of the
coexistence of opposites. The reed, with its pale exterior and empty
interior, would seem to symbolise the body, and the minstrel's
breath, the soul. The lamentations of the nay played by the
dervishes during their sessions of *dhikr*, 'the repetitive invocation of
God', evoke the lamentations of the soul when separated from its
divine source and its hope of returning there. Thus Jalal-ud-Did-
Rumi, the great Sufi master, said: 'We are the nay, and the melody
comes from Thee.'

82

you will dog the shadow of him who is led
    astray by his thoughts.

In the forest there is no sadness,
nor even grief.
When a breeze begins to blow
it carries no venom.
The sadness of the soul is no more than a shadow of
    illusion
that cannot last.
In the troubled sky of the soul
there are always gleams of sunlight.

Give me the nay and sing,
for song puts misfortunes to flight;
the laments of the nay will endure
far beyond the end of Time.

Rare are those who accept their life gladly,
without ennui condemning them to it.
So man has poured the river of life into goblets
    of illusion,
which, if he fills them to overflowing, inebriate
    him.
For a man drinks to find delight,
as though hostage to his passion, as though born
    addicted to drunkenness.
Thus, some drink in order to pray, others to
    covet riches
and yet others to find the stuff of their dreams.
Earth is a tavern kept by destiny:

the only blessed ones are those who find
  intoxication there.
And if you meet a sober man, let that surprise
  you.
Would the moon seek shelter beneath a stormy
  sky?

In the forest no drunkenness
comes from wine or from dreams;
for rivers contain only
an elixir of clouds.
Rather, drunkenness is a mother's breast whose milk
  nourishes man;
when he grows old and dies, then is he weaned.

Give me the nay and sing,
For song is the nectar in all our potions.
The laments of the nay will endure
far beyond the crumbling of mountains.

With man, religion is a field
tilled only by those who sow it with selfish
  prayers—
whether preachers hoping for eternal happiness
or ignorant men who fear the flames of hell.
Without the penalty of Judgement
man would not have worshipped any Lord
and without the promise of reward he would
  have blasphemed,
as though religion were a business matter:

devotion to its cause will bring him gain;
    neglect, loss.

In the forest there is no religion,
no hideous blasphemies;
for when the nightingale sings
he is not saying: 'This is just.'
The religion of man appears
like a shadow, then disappears.
After God and the Messiah
there is no religion on earth.

Give me the nay and sing,
for song is the pearl of prayers;
the laments of the nay will reach
far beyond the fading of Life.

If they heard talk of it, justice on earth would
    make the jinn weep;
and if they could see it, the dead would laugh.
For those who commit a misdemeanour are
    reserved prison and death;
and those who commit great crimes earn
    prosperity and fame.
The man who steals a flower is censured and
    scorned,
while he who robs the fields is a daring and
    fearsome hero.
He who murders the body is condemned to
    death,

while he who murders the soul remains
   unknown to all.

In the forest there is no justice,
nor even punishment.
When the willow's shade lengthens over the ground,
the cypress does not say: 'What sacrilege!'
The justice of man is like snow—
once the sun sees it, it melts.

Give me the nay and sing,
For song is the justice of hearts;
the laments of the nay will endure
far beyond the ending of sin.

Love, among men, appears in many a guise—
most are like blades of grass without flower or
   fruit.
Love is often like wine: he who drinks a little
   finds himself replete,
while he who drinks too much courts danger.
If the progress of love is driven by the flesh
to a couch draped with intentions, love will kill
   itself
like a king who, betrayed and imprisoned by his
   own,
wishes to end his life.

In the forest are no creatures of lust,
claiming the nobility of love;
for if languor overtakes the bull
he does not say: 'This is indeed true love.'

Love, for man, is an illness
growing within his flesh;
and when youth has flown,
that pain will pass away.

Give me the nay and sing,
for song is the real true love;
and the laments of the nay will endure
far beyond all the beauties of this world.

If you meet a man with a passionate love for a
    woman,
he eats of his hunger and drinks of his thirst,
and people think he is mad, saying:
'What does he hope of this love, through being
    so patient?
Do his eyes bleed with love for that woman
whose beauty and talents are not so engaging?'
Know that these are ignorant men, dead before
    they are born;
how can they grasp the sense of the Creator's
    trial and essence?

In the forest there's no one to utter reproof,
nor even to observe.
If the gazelles begin to frisk
when they see the sun go down,
the eagle does not say:
'Oh, how odd!'
Only the pious, amongst humans,
will claim that this is strange.

Give me the nay and sing,
for song is the folly most sublime;
and the laments of the nay will endure
far beyond the austere and rational mind.

Know, too, that we forget the fame of
    conquerors,
but until the hour of the Deluge we remember
    the madmen.
Slaughter spread through the heart of Alexander
    the Great,
and as Qays* breathed his last a proud temple
    rose up.
Thus the former's victories concealed defeat,
while triumph hid within the latter's losses.
Love is grasped in the mind and not in the
    body,
just as wine serves for inspiration, not for
    drunkenness.

In the forest, the only memories
are those of the suitors.
The men who enlarged their kingdoms
and oppressed the peoples of the world
are now mere names
in the list of criminals.
With us it is only the passion for slander
that is called gross injustice.

---

*Qays is a character from classical Arabic poetry, known for his
passionate love for Layla, like that of Tristan for Isolde and Romeo
for Juliet.

Give me the nay and sing,
and forget the cruelty of tyrants;
for the lily's cup is for dew,
not for torrents of blood.

What is happiness in this world, if not a mirage
    so deeply desired!
No sooner is it real than men grow tired of it—
like a spring rushing towards the plain
which, once there, becomes a torpid river of mud.
Man finds delight only in his feverish haste to
    seize
the forbidden fruit; and when he succeeds, at
    last he grows calm.
If you meet a man living happily away from that
    fruit,
know that he merits acclaim for every virtue.

In the forest there is no desire,
nor even weariness;
how can the forest wish for a partner
when it possesses all it needs?
What use is hope in a forest,
when the forest is hope itself?
And there is another reason:
life is hope itself.

Give me the nay and sing,
for song is fire and light;
and the laments of the nay are burning desires
that moderation cannot forbid.

The soul's design is concealed in its depths—
no words nor image can define it.
Some say: 'When the soul attains the limits of
    perfection,
it fades away, its mission accomplished.'
As though it were a fruit that ripens,
then, when the wind rises, falls from the tree.
And others add: 'When the body rests in peace,
there is no sleep nor waking left in the soul.'
As if the soul were a shadow over a pool—
when the water is ruffled the shadow vanishes,
    leaving no trace.
Yet everyone is led astray. For the essence will
    not
be buried with its body nor die with its soul.
Each time the north wind tangles the fringes of
    a spirit
the east wind rises and unravels them.

In the forest no difference exists
between body and soul,
for the air is idling water
and the dew is water at rest;
scent is a flower that opens,
a precious stone is a flower turned to crystal.
The poplar's shadow is no other than a poplar
which, thinking that night has fallen, has gone to
    sleep.

Give me the nay and sing,
for song is harmony of body and soul;

and the laments of the nay will endure
far beyond all dusk, all dawn.

The body is womb to the soul; there it remains
    till maturity,
then rises up, and the body is buried;
the soul is thus the embryo. And what is the day
    of death
if not the day of birth, with no miscarriage or
    Caesarian section?
Yet within man there are evil spirits
destined to be sterile bows no string can stretch.
The soul is the very quintessence,
conceived neither by the desert sand nor the
    muddy earth.
How many plants on earth are deprived of
    perfume,
and how many clouds, beyond the horizon, are
    empty of rain!

In the forest there is no sterility
or even adoption.
Inside a date there is a stone
which holds the secret of the palm-tree;
and in the honeycomb
lies hidden the symbol of beehive and fields.
Sterility signifies
nothing other than lethargy.

Give me the nay and sing,
for song is fluid;

and the laments of the nay will endure
far longer than all the monsters and hybrids.

Death on earth is an end for the son of the earth;
and for the son of the upper air, it is birth and
　victory.
He who embraces the dawn in his dreams will
　survive;
he who sleeps all night long will vanish;
and he who, as soon as he wakes, clings to the
　earth
will embrace it till Venus is no more.
Death is like the sea—he who is light will
　traverse it,
while he who carries the millstone of matter will
　founder.

In the forest there are no tombs,
nor even deaths;
for when April is over,
joy does not truly die.

The spectre of death is an illusion
that fades away in the heart.
To live through the springtime
is to live for ever.

Give me the nay and sing,
for song is the secret of eternity;
and the laments of the nay will endure
far beyond the end of existence.

Give me the nay, sing
and forget all that we two have said;
words are no more than dust,
so tell me, rather, of your deeds.

Have you, like me, left palace life behind
and chosen to live in the forest,
following the streams
and climbing the rocks?

Have you bathed in the fragrance of nature?
And dried yourself with the light of day?
Have you been drunk with the dawn,
in goblets of pure air?

Have you, like me, sat at dusk
among the vine stocks,
the grapes hanging
like lamps of gold?

To the parched these are spring water,
and to the hungry, food;
but they are fragrance and honey, too—
even wine, for him who wants it.

Have you lain on the grass at night
and covered yourself with the heavens,
renouncing the future,
forgetful of the past?

The silence of the night is a sea
whose waves break within your ears.
And in the bosom of the night is a heart
that beats in your bed.

Give me the nay and sing,
unmindful of troubles and cures.
For each man is nothing more
than a word written in water.

Heart and Husk

I have never drunk a cup of gall without finding the dregs were honey.

I have never climbed a steep hill without reaching a verdant plateau.

I have never lost a friend in the evening mist without finding him in the clear light of dawn.

And how often have I concealed my pains and fevers behind the veil of patience, believing this would bring me forgiveness and reward! Yet when I drew the veil aside I found the pains transformed into blessings and the fevers made cool and calm.

And how often have I walked with a companion in the visible world, saying to myself: 'How stupid and clumsy he is!' But as soon as I reached the hidden world you found me despotic and tyrannical, and him, serious and graceful.

And how often was I drunk on the wine of *self*, and you took my companion and me for wolf and ewe! And as soon as I was sober you saw us as two human beings.

O people, you and I are in love with what is

apparent in our state, blind to what is hidden within our truth. If one of us falls, we describe him as despicable; and if he walks with little steps we treat him as a decrepit old man. If he stammers he regard him as dumb; and if he utters a sigh we assume it is a death rattle.

You and I are passionately fond of the husk of the *me* and the superficialities of the *you*; that is why we see neither what the spirit has concealed in the *me* nor what is buried in the *you*.

What can we do, since, consumed as we are with vanity, we are unconcerned about what is true in us?

I tell you—and perhaps my words mask the face of my truth—I tell you as well as myself: what we see with our own eyes is nothing other than a cloud concealing what we should perceive with our inner sight, while what we listen to with our ears is merely a ringing sound disturbing what we should understand with our hearts. When we see a man being taken to prison by a police officer let us not hasten to assume he is a wrong-doer. When we see a corpse, and a man standing beside it with bloodstained hands, let us not conclude that this is a victim and his assassin. When we hear one man singing and another lamenting, let us ascertain which one of the two is truly happy.

No, my brother, do not look for the truth about a man in what he lets others see, and do not take what he says or does as the indicator of his inner-most thoughts. A man's clumsy talk and colourless style may lead you to think him ignorant, but his consciousness is often the art of thinking and his heart a receiver of oracles. As for the man whose hideous face and pitiful state lead you to despise him, he is often one of those heaven-sent gifts and, among humans, one of the inspirations of God.

If one day you visit people who live in a palace and others who live in a hut, you will leave the former in admiration and the latter in pity; but if you could tear the fabric woven by your senses from mere appearances, your admiration would fade and sink into despair while your pity would be transformed into veneration.

If in the course of the day you meet two men, one of whom lets you perceive the howling of the wind in his voice and the menace of the warrior in his gestures, while the other, fearful, utters broken words in quavering tones, you will see the former as strong and brave and the latter as weak and cowardly. But if you could see them confront difficulties or die as martyrs for a principle, you would understand that idle boasting is not courage, any more than silent timidity is cowardice.

If you see through your window a nun passing by on your right and a prostitute on your left, you will say at once: 'How noble is the former and how vile the latter!' But if you were to close your eyes for a moment and listen carefully, you would hear a voice whispering these words into the ether: 'The former praises Me through prayer and the latter beseeches Me through suffering, and each of their souls gives shelter to My spirit.'

Suppose you scour the world in search of what you call civilised and developed countries, and you enter a city full of great palaces, sumptuous institutions and wide streets, you will find the inhabitants rushing hither and thither, some of them digging the soil, others hovering in space, yet others investigating lightning or interrogating the air—and all dressed in elegant clothes as though attending a festival or fair.

A few days later you reach another city, where the houses are wretched and the streets narrow; if rain pours down on them from above these districts will turn into islands of clay in a sea of mud, and if the sun shines over the city it will become a cloud of dust. As for its inhabitants, they go on living between instinct and simplicity, like a slack cord between the two ends of a bow. They move about slowly and work in listless fashion; and it might be said that behind their eyes as they gaze at you are other eyes, looking at something that lies beyond you. Sickened, you leave their country, secretly saying to yourself: 'The difference between what I saw in the other city and in this one is as great as that between life and the approach of death. In the former there is strength in the flow of the tide, in the latter there is weakness in its ebb. There, diligence is like springtime and summer; here, indolence is like autumn and winter. There, perseverance is like youth dancing in a garden;

here, failure is like old age stretched out on a bed of ashes.'

However, if you had been able to look at those two cities by the light of God, you would have seen them like two trees growing next to each other in an orchard. Your reflections about their truth would broaden until you could see what you imagined to be progress in the one as gleaming, ephemeral bubbles, and what you believed to be indolence in the other as a secret and unchanging jewel.

No, life has its being not in its outer husk but in its folds and creases; the world is visible not in its skin but in its innards; people are visible not through their faces but through their hearts.

No, religion lies not in what the temples reveal nor in what rites and traditions show, but in what is hidden within souls and in what takes shape within men's intentions.

No, art is not in what your ears hear as the notes and inflections of a melody, nor in the ringing of the words in a poem, nor in what your eyes see as lines and colours in a painting. Art resides, rather, in those mute and quivering intervals between the notes and inflections within a melody. In a poem it lies in what reaches you through all that has remained silent, peaceful and solitary in the soul of the poet; and in a painting, in what it inspires in you, so that in looking at it you will see something more remote and more beautiful than the painting itself.

No, my brother, days and nights cannot be reduced to their appearances. And I, who walk in the procession of the days and the nights, can only be judged in the words I address to you through the meaning that reaches you from the peaceful depths of my being. So do not regard me as ignorant before you have examined my secret self, and do not deceive yourself by taking me for a genius before stripping me of the self I have acquired. Do not say that I am miserly before seeing my heart, or that I am generous before learning what inspires my generosity. Do not consider me as a loving being until my love is revealed to you with all that it contains of light and of fire; nor as carefree, until you have touched my gaping wounds.

The Veiled Land

Dawn is here, so rise, *my soul*, let us leave
these dwellings where we have no friends.
What hope can there be for a plant whose
    blooms
are different from any rose or poppy?
How can a brand-new heart find harmony
with hearts filled only with decay?

Morning is here—it calls out, listen;
so let us follow its footsteps.
We are weary of a dusk that claims
the light of morning as one of His loving signs.

We have spent the whole of life in a valley
beneath the soaring spectres of torment.
And across its slopes we have seen the flight of
    despair
like a host of owls and snakes.
We have drunk our fill of suffering from the river
and swallowed poison in the vineyards.

We have worn patience like a garment but that
   soon caught fire.
Then we gathered its ashes to cover ourselves
and to make a pillow, which turned
to thorns and straw during our deepest sleep.

O land veiled long before Creation,
how can we beseech you, how can we find you?
What is this desert that lies between us and
   what is this mountain,
your high wall, and which of us two, *my soul
   or I*,
will be the guide?
Are you a mirage, or are you the hope
within the souls who want the impossible?

Are you the dream drifting in men's hearts,
the dream that fades when those hearts awaken?
Or are you those clouds floating over the sunset
before they sink into the sea of darkness?

O land of thought, O cradle
of those who worshipped truth and venerated
   beauty!
We can reach you neither by ship nor by any
   other vessel,
and least of all on horseback or by camel.
You are neither to east nor to west,
to south nor north.

You are neither high in the atmosphere nor deep
    down in the seas;
neither are you in the vast plains or on the steep
    pathways.
In the minds of men you are light and fire.
You are this beating heart in my breast.

The Many-columned City of Iram

'Dost thou not consider how thy Lord dealt with (the tribe of) A'âd, the many-columned Iram, the like of which was not created in the lands . . .'

Koran, 89: 6–8

'Only certain ones among my faithful will be able to enter there.'

Hadith

Introductory Note

After Chaddad ibn A'âd had conquered the entire world, he ordered a thousand emirs among the most outstanding men of A'âd to seek out a vast area of land rich in water and pure air, far from the mountains, where they could build a city of gold. The emirs set out in search of such a land, each one taking with him a thousand servants. As soon as they found the land and had marvelled at it, they asked the architects and builders to draw up a plan for a square city with a perimeter of eighty leagues. They dug the foundations to the depth of the wells and built walls of Yemenite onyx up to ground level. Then they constructed a rampart five hundred cubits high which they clad with sheets of

104

gilded silver, so that the edifice could hardly be seen in the sun's glare.

Chaddad had ordered the gold to be brought from mines all over the world, and had bricks made from it. He dug up treasures, and within the city constructed a hundred thousand palaces, according to the number of dignitaries in his kingdom. Each palace was built on columns a hundred cubits high made of topaz and rubies, all with gold scrollwork. Chaddad caused rivers to run between them, with streams branching off for the palaces and houses. The pavements were made of gold, rubies and other precious stones. He decorated the palaces with gold and silver plating, and planted along the river banks all kinds of trees whose branches were of gold, and whose leaves and fruits were of topaz, rubies and pearls. The walls of the palaces were coated with musk and amber. And he had a garden prepared for his use, cut from precious stones, in which the trees were made of emeralds and rubies and other stones. And in the trees he put many-coloured birds, some of which would hoot and others twitter.

Al-Cha'bi, *The Lives of Kings*

Place and time

A small forest of walnut trees, poplars and pomegranate trees surrounding an isolated old house, situated between the source of the Orontes and the village of Hirmil in the north-east of Lebanon.

An afternoon in July 1883.

Dramatis Personae

ZAYN AL-'ABIDINE of Nahavand, Persian dervish, aged forty, known as the Sufi.

NAGIB RAHME, Lebanese writer, aged thirty-three.

AMINA AL-ALAOUIE, known in these regions as the jinnee of the valley, but nobody knows her age.

The curtain rises to reveal ZAYN AL-'ABIDINE *lying on the ground, propped on his elbow, in the shade of the trees. With the tip of his stick he is tracing circles in the earth. A few moments later* NAGIB RAHME *enters the forest on horseback. He dismounts and fastens the reins of his horse to a tree trunk. Then he brushes the dust from his clothes and approaches* ZAYN AL-'ABIDINE.

NAGIB RAHME

Peace be with you, master.

ZAYN AL-'ABIDINE

And with you also. (*He looks away, saying to himself:*) Peace we accept. But as for the title of master, we do not know if we accept it or not.

NAGIB RAHME (*looking around inquiringly*)

Does Amina al"Alaouie live here?

ZAYN AL-'ABIDINE

This is one of her homes.

NAGIB RAHME

You mean, master, that she has another house!

ZAYN AL-'ABIDINE

She has countless homes.

NAGIB RAHME

Since this morning I have been searching and asking everyone I meet to show me where Amina al-'Alaouie lives. But nobody told me she had two or three houses.

ZAYN AL-'ABIDINE

That shows that since this morning you have encountered none except those who see only with their eyes and hear only with their ears.

NAGIB RAHME (*astonished*)

What you say could be true. But kindly be frank with me, master. Does Amina al-'Alaouie really live here?

ZAYN AL-'ABIDINE

Yes, her body sometimes lives here.

NAGIB RAHME

But you will you please tell me where she is now?

ZAYN AL-'ABIDINE

She is everywhere. (*He points to the east.*) As for her body, it moves among those hills and valleys.

NAGIB RAHME

Will she return here today?

ZAYN AL-'ABIDINE

She will return if God wills it.

NAGIB RAHME *sits down on a rock facing* ZAYN' AL-'ABIDINE, *and examines him at length.*

NAGIB RAHME
Your beard leads me to think you are Persian.

ZAYN AL-'ABIDINE
Yes, I was born in Nahavand. I grew up in Shiraz and studied at Neyshabur. Then I travelled the world from east to west, and everywhere I feel like a stranger.

NAGIB RAHME
Each one of us is a stranger everywhere.

ZAYN AL-'ABIDINE
No, in fact. For I have met thousands of men, and in conversing with them I have noticed that they were satisfied with their environment and familiar with those around them—turning away from the world, so as to know just one bit of it.

NAGIB RAHME (*astonished by his interlocutor's words*)
Master, a man is inclined by nature to love the place where he was born.

ZAYN AL-'ABIDINE
A man with limitations is inclined by nature to love what is limited in life. And he who is short-sighted rarely sees further than one cubit of the path he is treading or of the wall he is leaning against.

NAGIB RAHME
It is not given to each one of us to embrace the fullness of life. And it is unfair to demand of

those with poor sight to see what is distant and infinitely small.

ZAYN AL-ʿABIDINE

You are quite right, for it is unfair to expect grapes that are still green to yield wine.

NAGIB RAHME (*after a few moments of silence*)

Listen, master. I have heard people speak of Amina al-ʿAlaouie for years. And the tales told about her have impressed themselves upon me so deeply that I have decided to meet her, to question her about her secrets and her mysteries.

ZAYN AL-ʿABIDINE (*interrupting him*)

Could there be anyone in the world capable of knowing the secrets and mysteries of Amina al-ʿAlaouie? Could there exist a man who could cross the seabed as though he were walking in a garden?

NAGIB RAHME

I have expressed myself badly, master, and I beg you to forgive me. I certainly cannot penetrate the secrets of Amina al-ʿAlaouie. All the same, I should like to hear from her own lips the account of her arrival in the many-columned city of Iram.

ZAYN AL-ʿABIDINE

You have only to wait by the door of her dream. If it opens, you will achieve your aim. And if it remains closed, you will have only yourself to blame.

109

NAGIB RAHME
What do you mean by that, master?

ZAYN AL-'ABIDINE
I mean that Amina al-'Alaouie knows more about people than they know themselves. For with a single glance she can see what is hidden within their conscience, their hearts and their minds. Therefore, if she finds you worthy of talking with her, she will speak to you. If she does not, she won't.

NAGIB RAHME
What must I say and do in order to be worthy of hearing her?

ZAYN AL-'ABIDINE
It is useless to try to approach Amina al-'Alaouie by means of some deed or word. She will neither listen to what you say nor pay attention to what you do. Rather, she will hear with her inner ear what you do not say, and she will see with her inner eye what you do not do.

NAGIB RAHME (*his face showing signs of astonishment*)
How eloquent and beautiful are your words!

ZAYN AL-'ABIDINE
What I say about Amina al-'Alaouie is no more than the stammering of a mute struggling to sing a hymn.

NAGIB RAHME
Would you know, master, where this strange woman was born?

ZAYN AL-'ABIDINE

She was born in the bosom of God.

NAGIB RAHME

I mean the place where her body was born.

ZAYN AL-'ABIDINE

Near Damascus.

NAGIB RAHME

Can you tell me about her parents and her education?

ZAYN AL-'ABIDINE

Your questions are like those of judges and law-makers. Do you think you can grasp the essence of things by inquiring about their appearance, or succeed in knowing the taste of a wine merely by looking at the jar?

NAGIB RAHME

There is a link between the mind and the body, just as there is a relationship between the body and its environment. And since I do not believe in chance, I think that to reflect on this link and on this relationship would not be devoid of interest.

ZAYN AL-'ABIDINE

Your words fascinate me! You do not seem to lack knowledge. Listen, then. I know nothing about Amina al-'Alaouie's mother except that she died when her daughter was born. As for her father, Sheikh 'Abd al-Ghani, he was blind and known by the name of 'al-'Alaoui. He was the great master of esotericism and Sufism of his day. He was,

God rest his soul, very deeply attached to his daughter. He took care of her education and culture and passed on to her all he knew. When she reached maturity he realised that, in comparison with the innate knowledge that she had received from on high, the knowledge she had received from him was as infinitesimal as is spray in the eyes of the sea. At the time, he would say of her: 'From my darkness shines forth a light by which I can see.' When she was twenty-five years old, duty called on him to take her with him on a pilgrimage. After crossing the Syrian desert, three stages before Medina the blind man caught a raging fever so violent that he died. His daughter buried him at the foot of a mountain and for seven nights kept vigil over his tomb; there she conversed with his spirit, asking it to reveal to her the secrets of the hidden world so that she could learn what was beyond the veil. On the seventh night her father's spirit advised her to let her horse go free, to carry her belongings on her shoulder and proceed towards the south-east, which she did.

He stops speaking for a brief moment, scanning the horizon. Then he goes on with his story:

Amina al-'Alaouie continued into the desert as far as Rub' al-Khali, the heart of the Arabian peninsula, which no caravan had ever crossed and which only a few people had been able to reach from the dawn of Islam down to our time. The pilgrims believed she had lost her way in the desert and died of hunger. On their return to Damascus they spread the news, which saddened all those who had known the virtues of Amina al-'Alaouie and of her father. Then oblivion wiped out the memory of their names as though they had never existed . . . Five years later Amina al-'Alaouie reappeared in Al Mawsil. The sight of her radiant beauty, her noble bearing, her goodness and her knowledge was not unlike, in its effect, the fall of a meteorite. She walked among the people, her face unveiled, and took part in the meetings of the ulema and the imams, speaking to them of divine things and with matchless eloquence describing the many-columned city of Iram. When her reputation burgeoned and the number of her followers and disciples multiplied, the city's ulema feared both the emergence of a heresy and insurrection. So they denounced her to the vali. Summoning her, he gave her a purse full of gold and requested her to leave the city. She refused the money; and at nightfall she departed, taking no one with her. She went to Constantinople, Aleppo and Damascus, then on to Hims and finally Tripoli. And in each of these towns she stimulated what had been lifeless in people's souls and revived what had been extinguished in their hearts. They would gather around her and, drawn by some magic power, would listen as she told of her strange experiences. But the theologians and learned men in each of these cities, complaining to the governors, confronted her and denied what she said. Afterwards, her soul desiring solitude, she came to live in retirement here. That was several years ago. Here she led a reclusive and pious existence, interested in nothing except the profound study of the mysteries. This is only a minute part of what I know about the life of Amina al-'Alaouie. As for what I understand, through divine grace, of her spiritual self and of the harmony within her soul as between her powers and her talents, I cannot speak of it now. Who among men could collect in mere goblets the pure air that surrounds this world?

NAGIB RAHME (*moved*)

I thank you, master, for all you have felt able to tell me about this strange woman. You have redoubled my wish to find myself in her presence.

ZAYN AL-'ABIDINE (*gazing at him for a moment*)

You are a Christian, are you not?

NAGIB RAHME

I was born a Christian. However, I know that if we set aside everything that adheres to all religions in the way of denominational and social excrescences, we would discover that they amount to just one single religion.

ZAYN AL-ʿABIDINE

Precisely so. And no one amongst mankind knows as much about this absolute unity of religions as does Amina al-ʿAlaouie. For any man, whatever his faith, it is like the morning dew that falls from above in dense droplets of glistening pearls amongst the diverse shapes and colours of the leaves and flowers. Yes, it is like the morning dew . . .

He stops suddenly and looks towards the east, listening. Then he stands up and motions to NAGIB RAHME *to pay attention. The latter complies.*

ZAYN AL-ʿABIDINE (*whispering*)

Here is Amina al-ʿAlaouie!

NAGIB RAHME *puts his hand to his forehead, as though he had felt some change in the air particles. Then he looks and sees* AMINA AL-ʿALAOUIE *approaching. His features have changed and his innermost feelings are in disarray. But he remains rooted to the spot, seemingly petrified . . .* AMINA AL-ʿALAOUIE *enters and stops in front of the two men. In her countenance, gestures and apparel she is more like one of those idols worshipped by ancient peoples than a contemporary oriental woman. It is difficult to guess her age from a mere glance at her features. Her face, although youthful, seems to conceal a thousand years of knowledge and experience. As for* NAGIB RAHME *and* ZAYN AL-ʿABIDINE, *they remain motionless in reverential fear as though in the presence of one of God's prophets . . . After fixing* NAGIB RAHME *with a gaze that seems to pierce his breast,* AMINA AL-ʿALAOUIE *approaches him, her face serene, and smiles, saying in crystalline tones:*

O man of Lebanon, you have come to meet us, sensing our news and inquiring after our condition. You will find in us only what is in you, you will hear from us only what you have learnt from yourself.

NAGIB RAHME (*moved*)

Now I have seen, heard and believed. And I am overwhelmed.

AMINA AL-ʿALAOUIE

Do not be satisfied with little. For he who approaches the springs of life with one empty vessel will leave with two full to the brim.

She holds out her hand to him; with reverence and modesty, he takes it between both of his. Carried away by a secret force, he kisses her fingertips. She turns towards ZAYN AL-ʿABIDINE *and holds out her hand to him. He responds as* NAGIB RAHME *has done. Then she draws back a little and sits down on a carved stone in front of her house. Pointing to a nearby rock,* AMINA AL-ʿALAOUIE *says to* NAGIB RAHME:

Here are our seats—so take your place.

NAGIB RAHME *sits down, followed by* ZAYN AL-ʿABIDINE.

AMINA AL-ʿALAOUIE

We can see in your eyes one of the lights of God. He who looks at us with the light of God in his eyes sees our reality, naked and absolute. And we see in your face a curiosity

116

that your sincerity raises to the plane of desire
for truth. If there is a word forming on your
lips, say it and we shall listen. And if there is
a question in your heart, ask and we shall
answer.

NAGIB RAHME

I have come to learn about things that in-
trigue people through their strangeness. But
barely did I find myself in your presence than
I understood that life is none other than the
different manifestations of the universal
spirit. Thus, the same thing has happened to
me as to that fisherman who cast his net into
the sea in the hope of filling it with fish and,
when he pulled it ashore, found in it a purse
full of precious stones.

AMINA AL-'ALAOUIE

You came to question us about our visit to
the many-columned city of Iram, did you
not?

NAGIB RAHME

Yes, my Lady. Ever since my childhood those
few words, 'the many-columned city of
Iram', with all they contain of secret symbols
and images, have haunted my dreams and
dwelt in my imagination.

AMINA AL-'ALAOUIE *raises her head, closes her eyes and
in a voice that seems to* NAGIB RAHME *to emanate from
the heart of space, says:*
We did indeed reach the veiled city—we
entered, and we stayed a while. We filled our

117

mind with its fragrances, our heart with its mysteries and our garments with its pearls and rubies. He who denies what we have seen and known denies his own existence before God.

NAGIB RAHME (*slowly and cautiously*)

My Lady, I am only a child who wishes to express himself but can only stammer out his words. If I question you it is with veneration, and if I try to delve deeply into a subject it is with attention and sincere devotion. If my numerous questions were to impose upon your mystery, might your sympathetic feeling for me nonetheless intercede in my favour?

AMINA AL-'ALAOUIE

Ask what you wish. For God opens the doors of truth to him who knocks with the hand of faith.

NAGIB RAHME

Did you enter the many-columned city of Iram as a body or as a spirit? Is it a city built from crystalline elements found in the earth, and does it stand in a place known to the world? Or is it an ethereal city symbolising a spiritual state, to be attained only by the prophets of God and His saints when in that state of ecstasy that God casts over their souls like a veil?

AMINA AL-'ALAOUIE

The visible and the invisible on earth are

none other than spiritual states. I entered the veiled city with my body, which is my visible spirit, and I entered it with my spirit which is my invisible body. Anyone who attempts to differentiate between the atoms of the body falls into manifest disarray. For the flower and its scent are one. And the blind man who denies the colour and shape of the flower, saying: 'The flower is only a scent drifting through the air', is like a man with a cold who says: 'Flowers are only shapes and colours.'

NAGIB RAHME

So the veiled city that we call the many-columned city of Iram is a spiritual state?

AMINA AL-'ALAOUIE

Everything that is fixed in space and time is a spiritual state. Everything that is visible and everything that is intelligible are spiritual states. If you close your eyes and look into the depths of your inner self, you will see the world both as a whole and in detail; you will know in depth the laws it contains, the winding paths it follows and the roads that it explores. Yes, if you close the eyes of your body and open those of your spirit you will see the beginning of existence and its end—that end which in turn becomes a beginning, and that beginning which is transformed into an end.

Can any man see the absolute essence of life
by closing his eyes?

Any man can desire with an incessant and
ever-deepening ardour until that ardour re-
moves from his eyes the veil of appearances.
From then on he will see his true self. And he
who succeeds in seeing this self within himself will contemplate at last the absolute
essence of life. And is not every self the
absolute essence of life?

(*his hand on his heart*)
So everything within existence that is percep-
tible and intelligible can be found here, right
here in my heart?

Everything that is within existence itself is
found in you, through you or for you.

Can I say that the many-columned city of
Iram is within my essence but not within
existence?

Everything within existence is found within
your essence, and everything in your essence
is found in existence. There is no frontier
between what is nearest and what is most
distant, nor between what is highest and
what is lowest, nor again between the infinitely small and the infinitely great. In a single

drop of water reside all the secrets of the seas; and in a single atom, all the elements of the earth. In a single evolution of thought can be found every evolution and every system in the world.

NAGIB RAHME (*puzzled*)

I have heard it said, my Lady, that you travelled long distances before reaching the region known as Rub' al-Khali, at the heart of the Arabian peninsula. I have also heard that your father's spirit accompanied you, inspiring and guiding you as far as the many-columned city of Iram. Must anyone who wishes to reach this veiled city be in a state similar to yours and possess all the same physical and moral qualities in order to get there, as you did?

AMINA AL-'ALAOUIE

We did indeed cross the desert, suffering hunger and thirst, experiencing the terrors and the blazing heat of the day as well as the horrors and silence of the night before seeing the walls of the city of God. However, some people, without taking so much as a single step, had reached it before we did. They had known its beauty and splendour without experiencing bodily hunger or spiritual thirst. Yes, in truth, many of our brothers and sisters had visited that holy city without having had to leave their place of birth.

AMINA AL-'ALAOUIE *pauses and remains silent for a*

121

moment. Then she stretches out her hand, indicating the trees and the myrtles all around her:

Every seed that the autumn sows in the bosom of the earth has its own manner of separating the husk from the kernel and of making its leaves, flowers and fruit grow. But whatever the method, all the seeds have the same end: to stand before the sun.

ZAYN AL-'ABIDINE *sways backwards and forwards as though transported in spirit into a sublime world. Then he cries out in a melodious voice:*

Allah is the Most High. There is no other divinity than Allah, the Magnanimous, who casts His shadow between our tongues and our lips.

AMINA AL-'ALAOUIE

Yes, indeed. Say: 'Allah is the Most High. There is no other divinity than Allah, and there is nothing other than Allah.'

ZAYN AL-'ABIDINE *repeats these words in his heart, and* NAGIB RAHME *gazes at* AMINA AL-'ALAOUIE *as though bewitched, saying in a barely audible voice:*

There is nothing other than Allah.

AMINA AL-'ALAOUIE

Say: 'There is no other divinity than Allah and there is nothing other than Allah', and remain Christian.

NAGIB RAHME *bows his head and says these words in his heart before looking up, saying:*

I have done so, my Lady, and I shall repeat these words until the end of my life.

122

AMINA AL-'ALAOUIE

Your life has no end. You will continue to exist as long as everything endures.

NAGIB RAHME

Who and what am I, that I may continue to exist for ever?

AMINA AL-'ALAOUIE

You are yourself and you are everything. That is why you will continue to exist for ever.

NAGIB RAHME

I know, my lady, naturally, that the atoms of which my material unity is composed will continue to exist as long as matter exists. But will this idea that I call self last? Will this brief awakening girdled by sleep endure? Will those bubbles of foam that the waves hurl forth, sparkling in the sunlight, endure, when those same waves destroy them as they create others? Will those vows and hopes, as well as those sorrows and joys, perpetuate themselves? Will those illusions survive, trembling in that interrupted sleep, in that night so strange in its marvels and vast in its scope, depth and reach?

AMINA AL-'ALAOUIE *raises her eyes to the sky as though about to receive something from the black holes of the firmament, and in tones of affirmation, full of strength, knowledge and experience, she says:*

Everything that exists will endure. And its very existence is proof of its continuance. As for ideas, they are Knowledge in its totality; without them, the world would not have known whether it existed or not. Ideas are an entity this side of past eternity and beyond future eternity—a perpetual entity. It changes only to become more quintessential, disappearing only to reappear in an ever more brilliant image, and sleeping only in order to dream of an ever more sublime awakening. I am astonished when I see a man who affirms the permanence of atoms within the external trappings perceived by our senses, yet denying the purpose for which they were created. I am surprised when I see a man who attests to the immortality of the elements that make up the eye, yet doubting the immortality of the glance, which has taken the eye as its instrument. I am astonished to see a man confirming the perpetuity of effects yet declaring the extinction of causes. I am surprised to see a man preoccupied with all that is apparent and created yet turning away from Him who creates and makes apparent. I am surprised by the man who divides life into two parts so as to believe in the part that is passive and renounce that which is active. I am surprised by him who looks at these mountains and plains bathed in sunshine, who listens to the wind speaking the languages of the branches, who breathes in the scents of flowers and myrtles—and then says to himself: 'What I see and what I hear will never be destroyed, just as what I learn and feel will never be destroyed. However, that thinking spirit who becomes stupefied by what he sees, then contemplative; who becomes, as he listens, joyful, then melancholy; that feeling spirit who trembles, then grows expansive, and then, as he learns, loses hope but finally accepts—that spirit who embraces everything will disappear like foam on the surface of the sea, like a shadow in the light.' Yes, truly, I am astonished that a being can deny his entity.

NAGIB RAHME (*enthusiastically*)

I believe in my entity, my Lady. He who hears you speak and does not believe is more like a rock than a human being.

AMINA AL-'ALAOUIE

Although God has placed within every soul an envoy who guides us towards the light, some amongst us seek for life outside themselves. In fact, life is within them but they are unaware of it.

NAGIB RAHME

Might there exist, outside of us, insights without which we cannot reach our innermost depths? Are there not forces within our environment which draw *our* forces out of their torpor, and influences which waken that which is sleeping within us?

Hesitating, NAGIB RAHME *lowers his head for a moment, then adds:*

Did your father's spirit not bequeath to you things unknown to the prisoner of the body and to the hostage of the days and the nights?

AMINA AL-ʿALAOUIE

That is indeed so, but it is useless for the visitor to knock at the door of a house if there is no one within to hear and open to him. For man is a being who stands between the infinity within him and the infinity without. There is in us whatever exists in us— otherwise, what is outside us would not exist there. It is true that my father's spirit has spoken to me; for my spirit has called on his, which revealed to my external understanding what my secret understanding already knew. So without my hunger and thirst I would not have had bread and water. And without my ardent desire and my nostalgia, I would not have achieved their aims.

NAGIB RAHME

Is it given to each one of us, my Lady, out of our ardent desire and nostalgia to draw a thread with which to link our spirit to those which are liberated from their bodies? Are there not a certain number of persons endowed with the power of communicating with the spirits and transmitting their wishes and designs?

Between the inhabitants of the ether and those of the earth, as regularly as day follows night, take place dialogues by day and conversations by night. No man would fail to obey the will of the invisible forces gifted with reason. Numerous are the actions which the individual thinks he carries out by his own free will, whereas in reality he is destined to act as he does. How many great men in this world have gained their fame from their total submission to the will of one of the spirits, just as a lyre with subtle strings submits to the plucking of an expert musician? Assuredly, between the visible and the intelligible worlds there is a path that we take during the moments of ecstasy that we experience while unconscious. Then we return, with our spiritual hands full of seeds that we sow in the earth of our daily life and that will germinate in praiseworthy deeds and immortal words. Without these open pathways between our spirits and those of the ether, no prophet would have appeared to men, no poet would have arisen in their midst, no sage would have walked among them.

(*Raising her voice*) In truth I say, as the end of time is my witness: between the inhabitants of the beyond and those of this earth there are bonds similar to those that unite the commander with the commanded, the one who warns with him who receives the warning. We are surrounded by the desires that pull at our hearts, the intelligences that inform our understanding and the powers that awaken our strength. Our doubts do not weaken our obedience to what we doubt. Our surrender to the wishes of our bodies does not deflect us from what the spirits seek within us. Our blindness to our truth does not conceal it from the gaze of those who remain veiled. If we stop advancing, in fact we continue to do so by their progression. If we stop acting, in reality we continue to move through their motion. And if we keep silent we continue to speak through their voices. Our sleep does not banish their awakening within us, and our awakening does not divert their dreams from the scenes of our imagination. We and they are in two worlds encapsulated within one single world, in two states encompassed by one single state, in two existences united in one universal and eternal Consciousness. This Consciousness has neither beginning nor end, and no one can transcend its height or its depth; it knows no limits and escapes all direction.

NAGIB RAHME

Will the day come, my Lady, when scientific research and practical experience will show us what our spirits at present know only

128

through imagination, and what our hearts feel only through ardent desire? Will the survival of the spiritual self after death be confirmed to us as were certain secrets of nature, so that we can touch with the hand of abstract knowledge that which we touch at present with the fingers of faith?

AMINA AL-'ALAOUIE

Yes, that day will come. Yet how wide of the mark are those who understand an abstract truth with some of their senses, yet remaining perplexed until it reveals itself to their other senses. It is a very strange man who hears the blackbird singing and sees it fly, while still doubting what he sees and hears unless he can seize the blackbird's body with his own hand. It is a very curious man who dreams of a fine truth and then tries, in vain, to give it shape and enclose it within the confines of appearance, until finally he mistrusts the dream, denies the truth and suspects that very fineness. And it is an ignorant man indeed who imagines an object, conceives its shape and features and then, failing to prove it with superficial yardsticks and verbal proofs, considers imagination to be an illusion and concepts to be empty shells. But if he had examined the question a little and pondered a moment, he would have known that imagination is a reality that has not yet materialised and that concepts are a form of knowledge too sublime to submit to the constraints of measurement, too lofty and too broad to be locked into the prison of words.

NAGIB RAHME

Does reality truly exist in all imagination, and knowledge in all concepts?

AMINA AL-'ALAOUIE

That is truly so. The mirror of the soul can reflect only what appears before it; it would be incapable of doing otherwise, even if it wanted to. A lake at its calmest does not show you in its depths mountain tops, outlines of trees or cloud shapes that do not exist in reality; it could not do so even if it wanted to. The caverns of the mind do not send back to you the echo of voices that quiver in the ether but in fact cannot be heard, even if they wished to. Even if it wanted to, the light does not throw over the earth the shadow of an object that does not exist. For faith in a thing is knowledge of a thing. The believer sees with his spiritual vision what researchers or scholars do not see with the eyes in their heads, and through his innate ideas he grasps what they cannot understand through their acquired ideas. The believer experiences the holy truths through senses different from those employed by other men. The latter consider their senses as impenetrable walls, so they go on their way, saying: 'This city has no gate.'

AMINA AL-'ALAOUIE *stands up and moves towards* NAGIB RAHME. *Then, in the tones of one who wishes to say no more, she concludes:*

The believer lives his days and nights in their fullness. As for the unbeliever, he lives just a few seconds of them. Narrow indeed is the life of the one who, holding up his hand between his face and the entire world, sees only the lines on his palm. And he who turns his back to the sun and sees only the shadow of his body on the ground earns my deepest pity.

NAGIB RAHME *stands up, feeling the time of departure approaching:*

On my return shall I tell people, my Lady, that the many-columned city of Iram is a city of spiritual dreams, and that Amina al-'Alaouie reached it along the road of ardent desire and entered it through the gate of faith?

AMINA AL-'ALAOUIE

Tell them that the many-columned city of Iram is a reality and that its existence is like that of the mountains and forests, the seas and the deserts. Tell them that Amina al-'Alaouie reached it after crossing the desert and enduring the torments of hunger and raging thirst, as well as the distress that is born of solitude and the terror of isolation. Tell them that the titans of eternity constructed the many-columned city of Iram with what crystallised and became quintessential in the elements of existence. It is not they who have concealed it from men, but men who have veiled their souls so as not to see it. He who goes astray on his journey there should complain not of the difficulties and intricacies of the path, but of his guide and of his camel's driver. Tell people that he who does not light his lamp will see in the darkness only darkness.

She raises her head towards the sky and closes her eyes. Her features appear veiled in tenderness and grace. NAGIB RAHME *approaches her, his head lowered, remaining silent for a moment. Then he kisses her hand, murmuring:*

The sun is about to set. I must return to the dwellings of men before darkness envelops the road.

AMINA AL-'ALAOUIE

Go in the light, and may God be with you.

NAGIB RAHME

I shall go in the light of the torch you have placed in my hand, my Lady.

AMINA AL-'ALAOUIE

Walk in the light of truth that the winds can never extinguish.

She looks at him for a long time, her gaze full of maternal light. Then she turns and walks away through the trees until she disappears from sight.

ZAYN AL-'ABIDINE (*approaching* NAGIB RAHME)
Where are you going now?

132

NAGIB RAHME

I am going to friends who live near the source of the Orontes.

ZAYN AL-'ABIDINE

May I come with you?

NAGIB RAHME

With great joy. But I thought you would be staying near Amina al-'Alaouie. My spirit has placed you among the ranks of the blessed, and I would have liked to be in your place.

ZAYN AL-'ABIDINE

We live by the light of the sun, but at a distance. Who among us can live in the sun? (*In a voice charged with deep meaning:*) I come each week to receive her blessing and refresh my spirit. And when evening comes I desire nothing more, and go away satisfied.

NAGIB RAHME

I wish that all men would come each week to receive her blessing and refresh their spirits, and that they would go away fulfilled and at peace.

He unties the reins of the horse and leads it away, walking beside ZAYN AL-'ABIDINE.

Curtain

O Soul

Were it not my ambition to find eternity,
I would not have learnt the melody sung by the
ages.
I would have been forced, rather, to end my life,
so that my visible self would have secretly
withered and died.

O soul, had I not cleansed myself with tears,
had not my lids been shadowed with sorrows,
I would have lived with scales upon my eyes,
like a blind man, seeing only the face of
darkness.

O soul, what is life if not a night
fading until it ends in the dawn; and the dawn
endures.
And in the thirst of my heart is a sign,
proclaiming the existence
of a celestial river in the urn of death, womb of
clemency.

O soul, some madman may tell you: 'The soul
dies like the body,
and whatever passes from life to death surely
does not return.'
Then make this answer: 'Flowers die, but the
seeds remain.
And within them dwells the very essence of
eternity.'

Perfection

You ask me, my brother, when man will attain perfection.

So here is my reply:

Man will be on the path to perfection when he feels that he is one with space that knows no bounds and with the ocean that has no shores; when he becomes that undying fire, that ever-gleaming light, that still air or that violent storm, those clouds charged with lightning, thunder and rain, those rivers merry or sad, those trees in bloom or shedding their leaves, those lands that rise up into mountains or slope down into valleys, those fields under seed or lying fallow.

When man has experienced all this he is half-way there. And if he aspires to the summit of perfection he must, when he feels the fullness of his being, embody the child dependent on his mother, the father responsible for his family, the young man wavering between his aspirations and his yearnings, the old man struggling against his past and against his future, the devout man in his hermitage, the criminal in his jail, the scholar among his books and writings, the ignorant man adrift in the blindness of his nights and the darkness of his days, the nun poised between her blossoming faith and her thorny austerity, the prostitute caught between her gnawing weakness and the claws of need, the pauper strung between bitterness and submission, the rich man between ambition and kindness, the poet between the mistiness of dusk and the gleam of his dawns.

When man succeeds in experiencing and knowing all this, he achieves perfection and becomes one of the shadows of God.

The Soul

. . . The God of gods parted a soul from Himself and made of it a marvel.

He gave it the gentleness of the dawn breezes, the scent of wild flowers and the grace of moonlight.

He offered it a cup of joy, and said: 'You will drink from it only when you forget the past and cease to be troubled about the future.' And he offered also a cup of sadness, saying: 'As soon as you drink from it you will grasp the true essence of the joy of life.'

He breathed into this soul a love that would leave it at the first sign of satisfaction, and infused it with a subtlety that would abandon it with the first proud word.

He imbued in it a knowledge of heaven to guide it towards the pathways of truth.

He placed in its depths a perceptive eye that sees what cannot be seen.

He created within it a feeling that flows with shadows and moves with ghosts.

He had it wear a garment of burning desire, woven by angels in the iridescent hues of the rainbow.

He placed within it the darkness of perplexity, which is the shadow of light.

He took fire from the furnace of anger, raging wind from the desert of ignorance, sand from the shores of the sea of selfishness, and earth from beneath the feet of the centuries; and from this he moulded man.

He endowed man with a blind strength which breaks out in moments of madness and falls still in the face of his desires.

And he placed within him life, which is the shadow of death.

Then the God of gods smiled and wept. He felt a love which knew no bounds, and united man with His soul.

My Soul Abounds in its Fruits

My soul abounds in its fruits—will no hungry man come and gather them, to enjoy them to the full?

Is there no man fasting and avid for compassion who will break his fast by eating of my harvest, relieving me thus of the weight of my bounty?

My soul bends under the weight of gold and silver—will no one come and fill his purse and lighten my burden?

My soul brims over with the wine of ages—shall I not find a single thirsty man to take it and drink his fill?

Marvel at that man who, standing in the middle of the street displaying his jewels, calls out to the passers-by, begging them: 'Have pity on me, take what I hold in my hands. For pity's sake, take some.' But everyone passes by and no one turns round.

He would have been better off as a beggar wandering the streets, holding out his trembling hands to passers-by only to close them again, as empty as they are unsteady. It would have been better if he had been a blind man sitting on the ground, whom people pass without a glance.

Admire that rich and generous man who, after pitching his tents between desert and mountain, lights a hospitable fire every evening and sends his servants to comb the roads in the hope of their bringing back a guest whom he would receive with the greatest consideration. But the roads are empty; they offer no outlet for his gifts, no takers.

Better if he could lead the life of a beggar, of a pariah, wandering the town, his only worldly goods a stick in his hand and a bundle over his shoulder. And at nightfall he would join his fellow vagabonds at the street corners, taking his place beside them, sharing with them the bread of charity.

Marvel at the king's daughter who, as soon as she wakes in the morning, dons her crimson cloak, her pearls and her rubies; then, her hair annointed with musk and her finger-nails with ambergris, she goes out to walk in the garden where the dewdrops sparkle on the hem of her gown. And in the still of the night she goes out again to walk in her Eden in search of her suitor, but in her father's kingdom there is no one to love her.

Better for her if she had been a peasant's daughter, taking her father's sheep to graze in the valleys. She would have returned to her hut in the evening, her feet dusty from the steep paths, and the folds of her dress vine-scented. And when night fell and sleep reigned, she would have slipped away to meet her beloved.

Better for her to have been a nun living in a convent, her heart burning like incense, its fragrance spreading through the air; while her spirit would have been consumed like a candle, the upper air carrying its light aloft. When she knelt down to pray, the spirits of the invisible world would have carried her prayers into the caskets of the ages, which preserve the prayers of the pious along with the fervour of lovers and the thoughts of the solitary.

Better for her to have been an old woman sitting in the sun remembering those who had shared her youth, instead of being the daughter of a king in whose kingdom there is no one to consume, like bread and wine, her heart and her blood.

My soul abounds in its fruits—will no hungry man come and gather them, to enjoy them to the full?

My soul overflows with its wine—is there no thirsty man who would come and take it and drink his fill?

Let me be a tree that bears neither flower nor fruit. For the pain of fertility is more bitter than that of sterility, and the suffering of a rich man who seeks to give but finds no one to receive is more terrible than a pauper who begs but finds no one wanting to give.

Let me be a dry well into whose depths passers-

142

by throw stones. For that is less hard to bear than being a spring of fresh water offered to the parched, who pass by without seeking to drink.

May I be a broken reed trampled underfoot. For that would be better than being a lyre with silver strings in a home where the master's fingers have been severed and whose children are deaf.

My Soul has Taken me to Task

My soul has taken me to task and taught me to love what others reject and to treat as a friend the one whom they insult. And it has revealed to me that the power of love is not within the lover but in the beloved.

And before my soul took me to task, love within me was a slender thread stretched between two stakes placed close together. But now it has been transformed into a halo whose beginning and end are one, encircling all that exists, extending slowly to embrace everything that will ever exist.

My soul has taken me to task and taught me to see beauty beyond shape, colour and skin, and to contemplate things that people call hideous until they appear pleasing to me.

And before my soul took me to task, I saw beauty in flames flickering inside columns of smoke. But today the smoke has dispersed and now I see only the fire.

My soul has taken me to task and taught me to

listen to voices that come neither from tongues nor from throats.

And before my soul took me to task I was hard of hearing; I heard only tumult and uproar. But now I am all ears, listening to the silence and its choirs singing the hymns of time, intoning the praises of the firmament, revealing the secrets of the invisible.

My soul has taken me to task and taught me to drink what can neither be pressed into juice nor poured into goblets, which can neither be lifted by hands nor brushed by lips.

And before my soul took me to task my thirst was an ember hidden in a mound of ash that I extinguished with a handful of water from the stream or with a mouthful of wine from the press. But today my burning desire has become my goblet, my thirst is my drink and my solitude my intoxication. I cannot, never shall be, assuaged; yet from this inextinguishable fever rises an ecstasy that has no end.

My soul has taken me to task and taught me to touch what can be neither embodied nor crystallised; it has taught me that what we sense is only half of what is intelligible, and that what we grasp is a mere part of what we desire.

And before my soul took me to task I contented myself with what was hot when I was cold, with what was cold when I was hot and with what was tepid when I was warm. But now my points of contact are scattered and have turned into a thick mist moving through everything apparent in existence to mingle with everything concealed within in.

My soul has taken me to task and taught me to breathe air that neither myrtles nor incense can emit.

And before my soul took me to task, when I felt an urge to smell perfumes I would go in search of gardens, amphorae or incense burners. But today I can breathe in what can be neither burnt nor poured. I fill my lungs with exquisite scents that have never floated over the orchards of this world nor been borne through space.

My soul has taken me to task and taught me to reply, 'Present' to the summons from the fearsome unknown.

And before my soul took me to task, I would turn only at the sound of a voice I knew; I walked only along paths I had tried and found convenient. But now the known has become a steed that I spur on towards the unknown, while convenience is a ladder that I climb to reach what is fearsome.

My soul has taken me to task and taught me not to measure time by the yardstick of yesterday or tomorrow.

And before my soul took me to task I believed that the past was a time to which I could not return and the future a time I could not reach. But today I know that the present moment embraces the whole of time along with all it contains of aspirations, actions and achievements.

My soul has taken me to task and taught me not to limit space with the words 'here', 'there', 'down below'.

And before my soul took me to task I had the impression, wherever I went, of being far from all other points on earth. But now I know that every spot on which I stand contains every place, and that the route I am taking admits of all distances.

My soul has taken me to task and taught me to keep awake when the inhabitants of the neighbourhood are sleeping and to fall asleep when they wake.

And before my soul took me to task I did not see their dreams in my sleep, neither could they see mine while they slept. But today I never drift in my sleep without their seeking to observe me, nor do they fly in their dreams without my rejoicing at the sight of their liberation.

My soul has taken me to task and taught me to be neither proud if I am praised nor sad if I am rebuked.

And before my soul took me to task I was always doubtful about the value and scope of my work until the day when it was acclaimed or denigrated. But now I have learnt that the trees flower in spring and bear their fruit in summer without seeking praise, that they shed their leaves in autumn and go naked in winter without fear of disapproval.

My soul has taken me to task and convinced me

that I am neither larger than a pygmy nor smaller than a giant.

And before my soul took me to task I believed that humanity was divided into two species: the weak whom I pitied or ridiculed, and the strong whom I followed or rebelled against. But today I have learnt that I am one individual among the community of mankind. In fact my elements are their elements, in the same way that my thoughts, tendencies and aims are theirs. Therefore, if they make a mistake it is I who will have made it, and if they do some worthwhile deed I shall be proud of it; if they climb, then I shall climb with them; and if they take a step back, I shall too.

My soul has taken me to task and has taught me that the lantern I carry does not belong to me and that the song I sing does not come from my heart. So although I walk in the light, I am not the light, and although I am a well tuned lute I am not the lute-player.

My soul has taken me to task, my brother, and it has taught me much. And your soul has lectured you and taught you just as much. So you and I resemble each other, the only difference being that I speak of what moves me deeply and in my words there is a certain insistence, whereas you know how to keep your secrets to yourself and your discretion implies a kind of virtue.

Yesterday

I had a heart that exists no more.
So now it is unburdened, and all those around
  are comforted.
This was a season of my life that passed
courting the Muses and languishing from love.
Love is like a star of the night
whose light fades when dawn comes.

The enchantment of love is an illusion that does
  not insist,
just as the beauty of love is a shadow that does
  not linger.
And the vows of love are a cloud of dreams that
  vanish
as soon as the robust spirit awakens.

How many wakeful nights have I spent in
  company with ardent desire,
watching it, to ward off sleep!
And the spirit of passion stood guard beside my
  bed,

telling me: 'Do not drowse, for sleep is
    forbidden.'
And my sorrows whispered in my ear:
'He who seeks ecstasy in love should not
    complain of suffering.'

Those are merely days long past, when my eyes
foretold my meeting with the spectre of sleep.
And take care, my soul, to say nothing
of that season and all that happened then.

As soon as the dawn breeze arose,
I was in raptures, singing and dancing.
And when the clouds poured water from the sky
I took it for wine, I filled my cup.
And with my beloved lying beside me, when the
    full moon rose
on the horizon I cried: 'O moon, are you not
    ashamed!'

All that was yesterday,
and all of yesterday has vanished like the mist.
My past is lost, forgotten
like a string of pearly bubbles shattered by a
    breath.

O sons of my Mother, if So'ad* should approach
    the young people
inquiring after a lover grown despondent,

*A character in classical Arab literature representing the beloved.

150

tell her that the days spent far from the eyes of
  his beloved
have extinguished the flame in his heart,
that the burning coals have been replaced by
  ashes,
that in the flight of memory the tear stains have
  vanished.

If she grows angry, do not augment her ire;
if she weeps, console her;
and if she laughs, do not be astounded.
For this is the way of all lovers.

Oh, how I yearn to know—
Has a beloved one ever returned?
Must my soul expect after this sleep an
  awakening
that will show me the face of my cruel past?
Will autumn hear the melodies of spring
while dead leaves collect about its ears?

No, my heart will know neither rebirth nor
  resurrection.
No, my sap can never rise again.
Neither can the harvester's hand bring life back
  to the flowers
after the sickle's blade has cut them down.

The soul has aged within my body,
seeing now only the shadows of years past.

As my inclinations are scattered throughout my
    being
they lean now on the crutch of my patience.
And my desires have left me, growing old and
    bent
before they even reach the age of forty years.

So this is my state; and if Rachel* asks you:
'What has befallen him?' tell her: 'Madness.'
And if she adds: 'Can it disappear? Will he be
    cured?'
Answer: 'Only death will cure him.'

*The beautiful wife of Jacob who had difficulty conceiving; her
name means 'ewe' in Hebrew and 'exodus', 'departure' in Arabic.
Jacob worked for fourteen years in the service of Laban, Rachel's
father, in order to earn her hand in marriage.

The Torments of Age

O time of love, youth has gone by
and the years have paled like a fleeting shadow.
The good old times have faded like a line
traced out by phantoms on a mouldering leaf.
And our days are now the prisoners of torment
in a life that knows little rejoicing.

The being we love has left in despair,
and lassitude has removed the one we desire.
Another, who once distressed us,
has vanished like a dream between darkness and
    dawn.

O time of love, remembering those years
will hope sing of the immortal soul?
Could sleep remove the imprint of that kiss
from lips whose rosy hue has gone?
Or will ennui make us banish and forget
the ecstasy of love, the ardour of embraces?

Will death stop the ears that heard

the moan of darkness and the songs of silence?
Will the grave blur the eyes that saw
the mysteries of the tomb, the secret that cannot
    be solved?

How often did we drink from goblets that
    glowed
in the cup-bearer's hand like flaming coals!

And how often have we touched those lips
where sweetness and crimson dwelt in harmony!
And how often have we declaimed poems
until the vault of heaven heard the voices of the
    souls!

. . . They have faded, those days past, as flowers
    fade,
when snow falls in the depth of winter.
All that the hands of the centuries gave so
    freely,
the hand of poverty has taken away . . .

If we had known, not a single night would have
slipped away between drowsiness and sleep.
If we had known, not a single moment would
    have been lost
between unconcern and sleeplessness.
If we had known, not a single second
of the season of love would have passed out of
    sight of the beloved.

Now we know—but after the heart
had murmured 'Arise and go.'
Thus we heard it and we prayed to Him,
when the grave cried out: 'Approach!'

The Beauty of Death

Let me sleep, my soul is drunk with love.

Let me be drowsy—my spirit has had its fill of days and nights.

Light the candles and burn the incense all around my bed. Scatter rose and narcissus petals over my body. Sprinkle my hair with musk. Pour perfumes over my feet. Then see and read what the hand of death has inscribed on my forehead.

Let me sink into the arms of sleep, my eyes are weary of wakefulness.

Play the zither and let the notes from its golden strings quiver in my ears.

Play the flutes and the nays, and weave their sweet melody into a veil around my heart that is impatient to stop beating.

Sing the [Syriac] hymns of Urfa and let their magical meanings unfold until my feelings flow into them. Then gaze upon the light of hope in my eyes.

Dry your tears, my companions, raise your heads as flowers hold up their stems at the coming of the dawn. See the siren of death standing like a pillar of light between my bed and space. Hold your breath, and listen with me for a moment to the rustle of her white wings.

Come bid me farewell, O sons of my Mother! Kiss my forehead with smiling lips. And may your eyelids kiss my eyes, may your lips kiss my eyelids.

Let the children approach my bed and let them gently touch my neck with their smooth, milky-pink fingers. Let the old people come near and bless my forehead with their stiff and withered hands. Let the young girls of the neighbourhood come near and see the shadow of God in my eyes, and hear the echoes of the eternal melody hastening to mingle with my sighs.

Here am I at the top of the mountain, my spirit drifting through the space of freedom.

I am far, far away, O sons of my Mother. The mountain slopes are hidden from my eyes by the mist. The valleys' depths have been swallowed up in the sea of silence. The streets and alleyways have been erased by the hand of oblivion. The meadows, the forests, the hills, have vanished behind white ghosts like spring clouds, yellow ghosts like sun rays, red ghosts like the veil of twilight.

The songs of the waves have died away, the rivers' melody has faded, people's voices are silent; I hear only the hymns of eternity accompanying my spirit's journey.

Free my body from this linen shroud, and bury me among lilies and jasmine.

Remove my remains from this ivory coffin and place them on a bed of orange- and lemon-blossom. Do not weep for me, sons of my Mother, but sing a song of youth and joy. Do not weep, O young girl from the fields—sing, rather, the songs of the harvest and the wine season.

Do not flood my breast with sobs and lamentations, but with your finger trace there the symbol of love and the sign of joy.

Do not disturb the peace of the ether with funeral orations and the last sacraments, but let your heart sing praises with me for the afterlife and for eternity.

Do not wear black at my funeral, but white, as at a betrothal.

Do not speak of my departure with tears in your voices—rather, close your eyes and you will see me among you today and tomorrow.

Lay me on leafy branches, carry me on your shoulders and with soft steps take me to a verdant cradle in the distant countryside.

Do not take me to a cemetery, for the crowd there would disturb my rest, while the bones' slow eroding would rob my sleep of its tranquillity.

Take me to a cypress grove, and dig a grave for me in that earth where violets and poppies cluster.

Dig a grave so deep that the mountain streams will not carry my bones into the valleys.

Dig an ample grave, so that the spirits of the night can keep me company.

Take off my clothes, bury me naked in the heart of the Earth and lay me gently on my Mother's breast.

Cover me with handfuls of earth and with iris, jasmine and wild rose seeds. They will germinate on my grave and breathe in the elements of my body. And so they will grow, wafting through the air my heart's perfume and showing to the sun the secrets of my hands; and they will bend with the breeze, recalling to the passer-by my dreams and inclinations of bygone days.

Leave me now, O sons of my Mother, leave me and walk away, as tranquillity moves through uninhabited valleys.

Leave me here alone and disperse in silence, as the almond- and apple-blossom float away on the April breeze.

Return home, and you will find there what death could not take from you or from me.

Leave this place; the one you seek is now far, far away from this world.

Sources

The writings in this book have been selected from French translations of the following works by Kahlil Gibran, originally published in Arabic:

Books
'Ara'is al-Muruj (*The Nymphs of the Valley*), New York, 1906.
Al-'Arwah al-moutamarrida (*The Rebel Minds*), New York, 1908.
Al-'Ajniha al-moutakassira (*Broken Wings*), New York, 1912.
Dam'a wa Ibtisama (*Tears and Smiles*), New York, 1914.
Al-Mawakib (*The Processions*), New York, 1919.
Al-'Awasif (*The Storms*), Cairo, 1920.
Al-Bada'i'wa-t-Tara'if (*Marvels and Curiosities*), Cairo, 1923.
   The edition used was *Complete Arabic Works*, Dar al-Houda al-wata-niya, Beirut.

Kalimat Jibran, an anthology edited by Abbot Antonios Bachir, Cairo, 1927 (the edition used was published by al-Dar al-moutahida, Beirut, 1983).

Articles and Letters
As-Sa'ih (daily newspaper), 15 December 1913, and 9 March 1914, New York.
Rasa'il Jibran, letters collected and introduced by Jamil Jabre, Beirut.
Rasa'il Jibran at-ta'iha, letters collected and introduced by Riyad Hnayn, Mou-assasat Naufal, Beirut, 1983.

Study on Gibran
Tauq Boulos, *La Personnalité de Gibran dans ses dimensions constitutives et existentielles*, doctoral thesis, University of Human Sciences, Strasbourg, 1984.